H for HERITAGE
MUMBAI

Celebrating
30 Years of Publishing
in India

H for HERITAGE MUMBAI

FIONA FERNANDEZ

Illustrated by Sumedha Sah

HarperCollins*Children'sBooks*

First published in 2023 by HarperCollins Children's Books
An imprint of HarperCollins *Publishers* India
Building No 10, Tower A, 4th Floor, DLF Cyber City, Phase II,
Gurugram – 122002

2 4 6 8 10 9 7 5 3 1

P-ISBN: 978-935-6997-92-9
E-ISBN: 978-935-6997-98-1

Cover illustration: Sumedha Sah
Cover design: Shamika Chaves
Author photo: Pradeep Dhivar

Typeset in Libre Baskerville and Charter Font Family by Pradnya Naik
Printed and bound at Nutech Print Services - India

HarperCollinsIn

*

Contents

❁ Advance Praise for H FOR HERITAGE: MUMBAI ❁

FIONA Fernandez's delightful book, H for Heritage: Mumbai is a welcome addition to the literature on this great city. Designed for young readers with clear, engaging text that brings forth each place or person, it also presents quirky and little-known vignettes that animate each story. Charming illustrations accompany the entries and make this book a 'must have' for every young Mumbaikar.
Tasneem Zakaria Mehta, managing trustee and director, Dr Bhau Daji Lad City Museum, Mumbai

FIONA Fernandez is a very special Mumbaikar. Over the years, several of which I have known her, her commitment to the people of this special city is inspiring. As a child growing up in the then 'Bombay', my bus route from home to school passed by many of the beautiful colonial buildings of this city. Over the years one realised that "Bombay's" heritage went way beyond that. This is what Fiona has covered in H for Heritage: Mumbai. She has showcased the architecture and the history and thus brought to all the importance of conserving our past. Most of all, she has created a book that children can read and understand. If we do not teach the younger generation the importance of our past, how can our heritage be protected and saved for future generations?
Brinda Somaya, founder-principal architect, Somaya & Kalappa Consultants, Mumbai, and urban conservationist

THIS precious book will serve as a reference tool to make young minds aware of the need to preserve their heritage, in their own city—a small step towards keeping Mumbai/Bombay in safe hands amidst rapid commercialisation. The engaging narrative helps in understanding their

origins in attractive ways. Sumedha Sah's charming illustrations bring the content to life.

Dr Pheroza J. Godrej, chairperson, Godrej Archives Council and advisor, Godrej Mangroves

SOME of us have been born and brought up in Bombay, watching the city transform (for better or for worse), into Mumbai. It doesn't matter what we call it. We love all versions of this wonderful city. This simple and quaintly illustrated book on its architecture, heritage, and culture creates an awareness of our past. Let's hope we can preserve it forever.

Brinda Miller, artist and honourable chairperson, Kala Ghoda Association

THIS book promises to take one on a journey through Mumbai's by-lanes, exploring the histories of major institutions and landmarks that have over the years contributed to its identity while also appreciating the little pieces of local history that are a part of our everyday lives. *Sabyasachi Mukherjee, director general,Chhatrapati Shivaji Maharaj Vastu Sangrahalaya (formerly The Prince of Wales Museum, Mumbai)*

CAMOUFLAGED under each letter of the Alphabet, this is a rich and delightful compendium of history and anecdotes, covering monuments and cafés, statues and gardens, birds and leopards, streets and rivers, profusely illustrated with charming watercolours and written in an engaging style to amuse and inform anyone, of any age, interested in the city.

Cyrus J. Guzder, chairman-managing director, AFL Private Ltd., trustee, The Asiatic Society of Bombay, Marg Foundation, and Urban Design Research Institute

MID-DAY has been able to make room for heritage articles even in the midst of urgent civic and crime issues because its newsroom has the talent, like Fiona Fernandez, to justify their relevance in the news food chain. Through a weekly column and continued local history coverage, she has kept the delightful antiquity of Bombay alive in mainstream journalism. Local history is dismally under-represented in school syllabi. H for Heritage: Mumbai steps in to close the gap.
Tinaz Nooshian, editor-in-chief, Mid-day Infomedia Ltd

FIONA Fernandez infuses a lively curiosity for Bombay/ Bambai/ Mumbai's plural histories into her delightful introduction to this metropolis. Astutely, she uses the Alphabet to share select figures, events, landmarks, neighbourhoods and institutions with her readers. Supported by intriguing asides and crisp illustrations, this book illuminates many sparkling facets of this jewel among the globe's cities.
Ranjit Hoskote, poet, translator and curator

FIONA Fernandez brings her expertise at research, her journalistic clarity of thought and her power of expression, to the book. Choosing her subjects with care she not only covers what a visitor to the city would ordinarily notice but gives the reader a glimpse into the method that governs the madness that is Mumbai.
Reena I. Puri, executive editor, Amar Chitra Katha

H for Heritage: Mumbai features some of the city's most iconic landmarks and presents the intricate details of each of these sites in a succinct yet fun manner. A must-read for anyone hoping to connect with the rich culture and history of Mumbai!
Shaheen Mistri, founder and CEO, Teach For India

FIONA Fernandez has brought Mumbai's heritage and culture alive through the pages of this interesting and much-needed book. A must-read for children to understand the history and heritage of our city.
Amrita Somaiya, founder, Kitabkhana

A book as charming as it is charmed by its subject, Fiona Fernandez gives us splendid evidence of this city's profound history and its genius for reinvention.
Siddharth Dhanvant Shanghvi, author of Loss

THIS book makes this fabled city's complex histories as "easy as ABC" in entries from "A for Asiatic Society" to "Z for Zaveri Bazaar". Its iconic and everyday buildings and places, diverse flora and fauna, and quirky, beloved, and notorious Mumbaikars come to life in Fiona Fernandez's insightful text and Sumedha Sah's engaging pen-and-ink drawings.
Mary N. Woods, professor emerita, Cornell University, and wannabe Mumbaikar

FIONA Fernandez brings a journalist's eye and a lover's heart to this nifty little handbook on the city of many names by a restless sea. Carry it around wherever you go, give it to the friend who's visiting and save yourself from the ignominy of having to say, 'I don't know' when someone asks who was Atmasingh Jesasingh Bankebihari...
Jerry Pinto, author of The Education of Yuri, Em and the Big Hoom

THIS is an extraordinary book about Mumbai's beloved icons—whether physical spaces like VT or the Borivali National Park, or legendary Mumbaikars like Busybee or Boman Kohinoor. For older Mumbaikars reading it will be an enjoyable trip down memory lane, but for the next generation, this book's intended audience, it will serve both — a vital

portal into its past and a ready reckoner of all they need to quickly see, appreciate and preserve!
Parmesh Shahani, author of Gay Bombay: Globalisation Love (Be) Longing in Contemporary India

ENGAGINGLY written by Fiona Fernandez and delightfully illustrated by Sumedha Sah this book has been conceived to attract and inform younger or historically unfamiliar readers, it imparts its knowledge easily and in an assured approachable manner.
Dr Christopher London, architectural historian, author of Bombay Gothic

FIONA Fernandez's meticulously researched book narrated in story form and beautifully illustrated by Sumedha Sah, belongs in every classroom and library in India.
Kavita Ezekiel Mendonca, poet, Family Sunday and Other Poems, Light of The Sabbath

AS a passionate Bombaywali / Mumbaikar, this is one book I consider essential gifting...the visuals and text make our vibrant megapolis come alive as never before...
Shobhaa De, author and columnist

Fiona Fernandez has created a virtual gateway to the city and all that captures its romance with its citizens and tourists.
Murzban F. Shroff, author of Breathless in Bombay, Waiting for Jonathan Koshy, *and* Third Eye Rising

This is a book that anyone can enjoy at any age, dip into or read start-to-finish and find something new and memorable every single time.
Ashok Banker, author of The Grief Queen's Daughter *(work-in-progress)*

MUMBAI is more than just its film industry. Here's a book that reminds us of the city's rich history, makes its iconic buildings come alive in a simple and illustrative way that make it accessible for young minds. Replete with stories of the biggest heist from a jewellery store, to the museum that was converted into a hospital, Fiona, a resident Mumbaikar and seasoned journalist regales us with her stories of her city's built and natural heritage in this delightful book.

Bahar Dutt, environment journalist

❁ Foreword ❁

THIS delicious A to Z chronicle of the life of the city that I grew up in reminds me of my mother, Jennifer, and how she taught me to see the city ... not just inhabit it. So much of what Fiona writes about, my mum got me to see as a child. But *H for Heritage: Mumbai* gets you to see deeper. And as you journey through the alphabet of Mumbai, discovering layer upon layer of the fabric of this city, you can't help but love it, even if you love to hate it! You realise there is so much more to discover. Fiona's gentle reminders to 'look up' and notice things we are otherwise blind to, and that reveals a whole new dimension to what you thought you always knew.

But this book does so much more than ask you to just see the city; it actually asks you to experience it and its indomitable spirit, which is exemplified in its ability to reinvent itself through the inevitable, by embracing change, disaster and success. Celebrating its resilient citizens and their spirit.

What better way to get children to love the idea of history than by getting them to discover their own city! And this is the most perfect companion towards that discovery. For children and adults alike ... let the journey begin!

— *Sanjna Kapoor, theatre person*

❁ Author's Introduction ❁

CIRCA 2004. Asiatic Society Library. 10.30 a.m.: A grouchy library assistant emerged from a dusty, labyrinthine corridor; his face partially hidden behind a stack of books that I had requested for. After two hours of poring over titles for a fact book on Mumbai, the penny had dropped. Call it serendipity but this moment occurred on my first visit to one of Mumbai's oldest libraries, the epicentre where the idea of this great city was possibly first discussed by some of its visionaries.

Like many from my generation, as well as those before and after mine, I was exposed to only a fraction of the city's history and heritage in textbooks. Successive years of research led to more realisations of this vacuum, and that there was more to our history apart from the seven-islands-one-city narrative. Stories emerged from decrepit landmarks, on lesser-beaten gullies, in the diaries of our founding fathers, and even in one of Asia's oldest cemeteries!

The big question emerged: Can history be relayed beyond intimidating accounts woven by a series of dates? The answer was my Eureka moment—Let's use the letters of the alphabet to introduce young minds to their city's origins and evolution. In *H for Heritage: Mumbai,* each letter will explore an important, unique location, milestone, landmark, or personality, shared in the form of pocket-sized accounts and intriguing, oddball trivia. I borrowed from Rudyard Kipling, who had famously said that history would never be forgotten if told like stories. Don't miss the exploits of this Nobel Laureate as a child in this book, among many unheard gems about Mumbai's famous and infamous, its indigenous and migrant communities, all of whom contributed to its enterprise and eccentricities, and its farsighted thinkers, who had big dreams for the city.

As you flip through, you'll notice that vast sections in the book refer to the city as 'Bombay' instead of Mumbai. This was necessary and critical to retain the historical continuity and context of the time period when it was known by that name, before it was officially changed to Mumbai in 1995.

The book, the first in a series that will feature other Indian cities, was also conceived to raise a timely voice about heritage conservation so the coming generations realise their role as custodians of this precious repository of living and tangible heritage. I hope to continue on this juggernaut with this series—of narrating history in the form of captivating stories.

I encourage not just children, but curious enthusiasts of all ages to pick this book to have an enchanted love affair with a city that is also an emotion.

For mum
Because you taught me the A-Z of life

A
for
ASIATIC SOCIETY

WHERE IN MUMBAI will you find a finely sculpted collection of statues that pay tribute to its earliest thinkers and administrators, and a library that stocks some of Asia's rarest books? From philanthropist Sir Jamsetjee Jeejeebhoy to visionary Governor Mountstuart Elphinstone, you'll spot their statues inside the Town Hall building which houses the Asiatic Society of Mumbai (previously Bombay). You need to climb thirty steps to enter what is possibly one of the most historic buildings in the city. But before you do so, look out for a stone slab at the base of the first step with '0' (zero) engraved on it. Known as the Town Hall datum, this represents the point at sea level. The Asiatic Society was founded in 1804 by James Mackintosh and sixteen other English gentlemen as the Literary Society, to create a platform where great minds could encourage the arts and sciences. It was the heart of intellectual thought and discussion in Bombay. The current structure, one of the city's earliest examples of neoclassical architecture, was designed in by Thomas Cowper. The Asiatic Society moved into the building in 1830. The site for this building was chosen because it is near the Mint, the Bombay Harbour and St Thomas Cathedral.

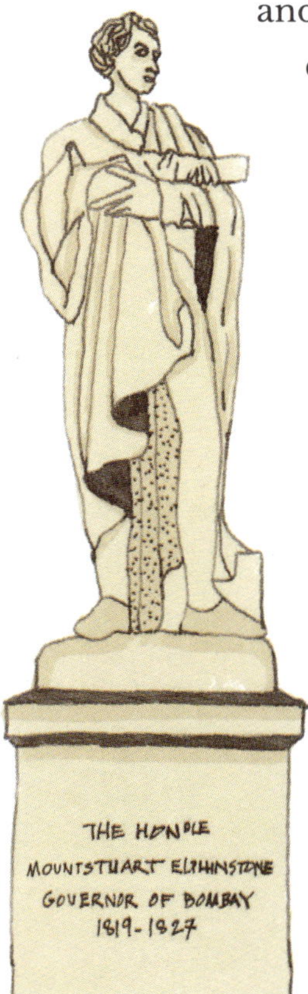

The Town Hall has been witness to several historic events—the first exhibition of electric lights in 1847; Lord Elphinstone's announcement of the Queen's Proclamation of transfer of power from the East India Company to the Crown in 1858; the first convocation of the University of Bombay in 1862. In 1948, grieving citizens paid their last respects to Mahatma Gandhi, whose ashes were kept here in an urn for public homage. It has hosted Western classical music concerts and theatre performances.

The Society's massive library is home to 2,000-plus manuscripts and over 2.5 lakh titles. It boasts of rare antiquities, artefacts, coins, maps and literature from not just English and Indian languages but also European languages, Pali, Sanskrit, Arabic and Persian. While the Town Hall was the seat of civic activity, the Asiatic Society was a centre for research and knowledge gathering. Their symbiotic association resulted in it becoming the nucleus for education, dialogue and debate in erstwhile Bombay. The Society has introduced awareness programmes and drives to encourage public participation in its conservation efforts.

If you're keen to learn about how the city grew from a cluster of islands to the Crown's most prized city, this is the best place to begin that discovery.

Where: Shahid Bhagat Singh Marg, opposite Horniman Circle Garden, Fort

---

A *for* Afghan Church: Land ahoy!

This church is actually consecrated as St John The Evangelist, but it earned this name because it was commissioned as a memorial for British soldiers who were martyred in the two Anglo-Afghan Wars (1839-42 & 1878-80). The tower and steeple (198 feet) of the Afghan Church were once the highest and hence most visible structures located at the tip of Colaba that served as landmarks for incoming ships sailing towards Bombay's harbour!

B
for
BOMBAY SAMACHAR

A STONE'S THROW away from the Asiatic Society, in the heart of the original city, you will spot a nondescript, red brick-coloured building. It houses Asia's oldest newspaper that is still in operation. The Bombay Samachar (renamed Mumbai Samachar), a Gujarati-language daily, has been in circulation since July 1, 1822. The newspaper was established by Parsi scholar and priest Furdonjee Marzbanjee, who is often hailed as the father and founder of the native press movement in India. It proved to be an instant hit among the Gujarati-speaking population in the city, many of whom had migrated from the neighbouring Gujarat. Another chunk of readers were Parsis and Iranian Zoroastrians, who also speak Gujarati. It was a weekly till 1832, continued as a bi-weekly till 1855, and has been a daily since then. It remains one of the most read newspapers among Gujarati speakers of West India. The Cama family has been running the paper since 1933.

Nearby, you will notice a beautiful circular garden and a semi-circular enclave. It was designed by James Scott in 1865 and the buildings were completed in 1873 to become Bombay's first planned business district. The garden was laid out in 1869. Both these landmarks were originally called Elphinstone Circle and Elphinstone Circle Garden (in honour of former Governor John Elphinstone). While there, look out for the keystone heads of men and women etched on each floor level of these buildings. The Circle and Garden were renamed in 1947 after Benjamin Horniman, the fearless, pro-Independence British editor of the English language newspaper, Bombay Chronicle, that was in publication till 1959. It was also printed by The Bombay Samachar Press.

Where: Bombay Samachar Marg, near St Thomas Cathedral, Fort

B *for* **Busybee: The original Bombaywalla**

Few knew him as Behram Contractor. But most referred to him by his pen name, Busybee, thanks to his popular column, Round and About, that he wrote for The Afternoon Despatch & Courier, the newspaper that he started in 1985. The affable Parsi journalist was one of the city's most loved newspaper entrepreneurs. Through his daily columns that appeared on the back page of the newspaper, he would regale and engage readers about the goings-on in the city and country in his inimitably witty style. While he was the narrator, fictional characters like The Wife, sons, Daryl and Derek, and his talking dog, Bolshoi the boxer, played key roles in his column.

B *for* **Banganga Tank: Water for a thirsty God**

Banganga Tank in Walkeshwar has a connection with The Ramayana. It derives its name from an account in the epic. Lord Ram was feeling thirsty while on his journey to Lanka to rescue Sita, and is believed to have struck an arrow into the ground here, leading to the emergence of a water spring. The water tank is considered a revered site frequented by devotees on auspicious days of the Hindu calendar. Conservationists have been working closely with local residents to protect this heritage landmark from neglect.

C
for
CHURCHGATE

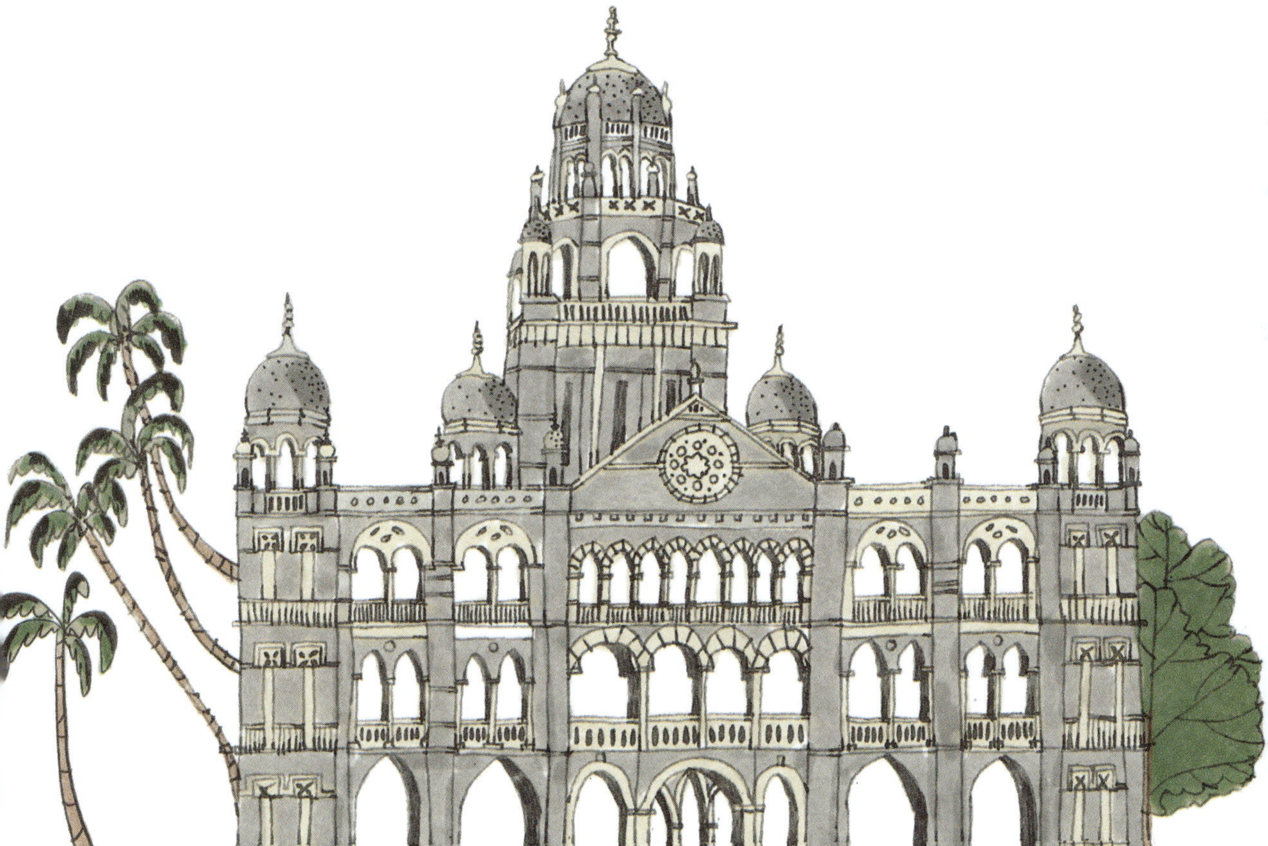

ONCE UPON A TIME, the British built a Fort with impregnable walls and watchtowers, and canons that were aimed towards the coast, in case of an enemy attack via the Arabian Sea. This Fort housed British settlements and military and administrative offices. Only a few Indian homes and establishments existed on its fringes. It had three gates—Bazaar Gate, Church Gate and Apollo Gate. Each of these gates was named after the area in which it was located. Of the three, the name Church Gate was inspired from the St Thomas Cathedral that is located near the spot where it is believed to have been built. As the population began to grow within the Fort, the farsighted Governor of Bombay, Sir Bartle Frere (term: 1862-67), ordered that its walls be brought down to de-congest the area and improve living conditions. Interestingly, many of the names connected with the Fort remain till date. The best example is the Churchgate building that housed the offices of Bombay, Baroda and Central India Railway (today's Western Railway). This building was opposite the Churchgate station. It was completed in 1899 by British architect F.W. Stevens and his eldest son, Charles, along with Rao Saheb Sitaram Khanderao Vaidya. The stunning white-coloured building is a combination of Venetian Gothic and Indo-Saracenic styles. The gates and the Fort are long-gone but the name has stuck. The building was made of white Porbandar stone, and has ornamental wood carvings that are quite spectacular.

If you step outside this landmark, turn to your left and look in the direction of Flora Fountain, you might actually be able to spot the top of the bell tower of this Cathedral, and relive your own moment from the past!

Where: Veer Nariman Road

C *for* **Crawford: Bombay's King Arthur**

Bombay's first municipal commissioner, Arthur Crawford (term: 1865-71), had many firsts to his name—including commissioning the city's first wholesale market that was named after him. Crawford Market was later renamed after Indian reformist Mahatma Jyotiba Phule. Designed by William Emerson via a contest, the covered structure, built in 1869, spreads across a mammoth 2.25 hectares, and accommodates fish, meat, fruit and vegetable vendors, as well as commercial goods traders till date. Crawford also gave the city its first electric streetlights that were called Crawford's Fireflies (because these bright lights attracted the fireflies). The first lights were installed in Esplanade, Bhendi Bazaar, Churchgate and its surrounding areas. The lit streets led to a drop in crime rates in those parts.

D
for
DALAL STREET

BEFORE ELPHINSTONE CIRCLE and its Garden (later renamed as Horniman Circle) were created, the site was called Bombay Green. It was an open ground where bales of cotton were piled up and auctioned. Cotton traders and stockbrokers would assemble here. In 1851, twenty-two stock brokers began trading under a banyan tree nearby. They invested a sum of Rs one, which was worth little even in those days. That group was called the Native Share and Stock Brokers Association.

Today, that banyan tree still exists, and stands witness to the foundation laid by those twenty-two traders. It was to become the Bombay Stock Exchange (BSE) on Dalal Street, a stone's throw away from this historic location. In 1874, the brokers found a permanent place and the area came to be known as Dalal Street or Brokers' Street. Asia's oldest stock exchange and the fifth largest in the world was officially formed in 1875 but since that time in the 1850s, brokers and traders mushroomed in the area, as Bombay experienced a cotton boom, indirectly aided by the American Civil War. Textile mills sprung up across the island city. While the boom went bust after that war, it benefited the city in many ways and set the tone for it to become India's commercial capital. These entrepreneurs, traders and merchants were mostly Gujaratis and Parsis, as well as the Sassoons, who were Baghdadi Jews. They channelled excess funds towards the city's infrastructure as well as for philanthropic causes like public buildings and utility services.

In 1956, the Government of India recognised the BSE as India's first stock exchange. The construction of the famous Phiroze Jeejeebhoy Towers (the current location of the BSE) began in the 1970s, and the BSE commenced operations in 1980. While it was initially called BSE Towers, following the death of Sir Phiroze Jamshedji Jeejeebhoy, chairman of the BSE, the building was renamed in his memory in 1966. Since 2002, it has been known by its current name, Bombay Stock Exchange.

Where: Bombay Stock Exchange, Phiroze Jeejeebhoy Towers, Dalal Street

D *for* Dabbawala: Code word for lunch

The world-famous dabbawalas of Mumbai have a huge fan following, including King Charles III, who met them on his visit to Mumbai in 2003. He even invited them to his wedding with Lady Camilla, Queen Consort of the United Kingdom. He, like many others, was fascinated by the unique alphanumeric coding system they follow to ensure the correct dabba (lunchbox) reaches its rightful customer. When their services began in 1890, they used different coloured threads on the dabbas for different areas across the city and suburbs. Later, when oil paint was available, coded symbols were used. The third generation of dabbawalas devised a coded system with numbers and letters of the alphabet. It also changed the language from Marathi to English for all users' convenience. The six sigma code is a combination of three elements—area code, dabbawala code and destination code. Every area/ suburb is differentiated with a different colour code (red, blue, green, yellow and so on) for easier identification.

E *for* ESPLANADE MANSION

" ... this Indian sham Quaker is just a rowdy, and is always noisy when awake—always chaffing, scolding, scoffing, laughing, ripping, and cursing, and carrying on about something or other ... Nothing escapes him; he notices everything that happens, and brings out his opinion about it, particularly if it is a matter that is none of his business."

Extracted from The Complete Works of Mark Twain: Following the Equator, Volume 2, Harper and Brothers: New York, 1925

THE GREAT AMERICAN author and creator of literary characters like Tom Sawyer and Huckleberry Finn came to Bombay to promote his writing. He made this observation on Indian crows that would gather in his balcony during his stay at the now-shuttered, neglected building that was one of Bombay's most popular luxury hotels—Watson's on Esplanade in Kala Ghoda.

This structure, built in the late 1860s, remains possibly India's only remaining cast-iron structure; the pre-fabricated maze of the building was actually shipped from England. It was designed, manufactured and shipped by British engineer Rowland Ordish. The architectural marvel, now referred

to as Esplanade Mansion, sadly lies in ruin since it is caught in a long-drawn legal battle. The court has barricaded the site as it has been deemed unsafe. Its tenants have vacated the space that had been reduced to a congested maze of occupants and mindless interventions. Conservationists, meanwhile, are hoping that it can be sensitively preserved by heritage experts. In fact, the building is part of the Victorian Gothic and Art Deco ensemble that won a UNESCO World Heritage Site tag in 2018.

In its heyday, in the early twentieth century, it was a high-class accommodation in Bombay for the rich and famous, and commanded great views of the Arabian Sea, Back Bay and Malabar Hill. The hotel boasted of the city's 'finest and handsomest' dining room, a grand orchestra that came to life for its ballroom extravaganzas, shopping arcades where customers were shielded from the sun and rain—a first for Bombay at the time—and a high-profile guest list that included the likes of Twain and M.A. Jinnah. By the 1920s, the Taj Mahal Hotel began to emerge as the more preferred and prestigious luxury hotel of Bombay. Gradually, Watson's fell out of favour; its owners changed hands and it got neglected, eventually bringing to an end its glory days.

Where: Mahatma Gandhi Road, Kala Ghoda

COOL FACT › INDIA'S FIRST EVER FILM SCREENING

The hotel became the first Indian venue where Frenchmen, Lumière brothers screened their short films on their cinematographe (projector) as part of their historic world tour in 1896 to introduce cinema to the world.

E *for* Elephanta Caves: Shifting legacy

Mumbai's first UNESCO World Heritage Site tag was given to Elephanta Caves in 1987. But do you know that the island was originally referred to as Gharapuri or Puri? It earned its current name because of a massive statue of an elephant that was originally located near the southern landing end of the island. In the late nineteenth century, it was noticed that the statue was beginning to degenerate, and so it was shifted to the lawns of Victoria Gardens (today's Veermata Jijabai Bhonsle Udyan, also known as Rani Baug) in Byculla. You can spot the massive stone statue near the entrance of the Dr Bhau Daji Lad Museum, which is in the same complex.

F
for
FLORA FOUNTAIN

IT HAS BEEN a long journey from the Isle of Portland in the United Kingdom to Bombay, a city that grew from seven islands. Flora Fountain was commissioned and built in honour of its visionary Governor, Sir Bartle Frere. His radical decision to break the walls of the original Fort proved to be a watershed moment in the city's timeline. When the fountain was assembled and placed on a square on November 18, 1869, it was called Frere Fountain, in his honour. It was later renamed after Flora, the Roman Goddess of Abundance. Scottish architect Richard Norman Shaw designed the fountain that was sculpted in imported Portland stone by James Forsyth. Both their names are inscribed on the south side of the third level tray.

Apart from the seven-foot-high statue of Flora, the lower tier of the white stone landmark has four statues seated in niches in the four corners, depicting women in four different attires. These symbolic women represent the industrial, cereal, plant and edible products of India. Also look out for cast iron lion-headed spouts, and dolphins. Standing at approximately thirty-three feet, Lady Flora watches over one of the city's busiest traffic signals where five of its most important roads meet.

Where: Mahatma Gandhi Road junction, Hutatma Chowk, Fort

F *for* Fort Stikine: When gold fell from the sky!

On April 14, 1944, the busy Bombay Harbour witnessed its most destructive explosion till date. The impact was heard across many parts around the city's southern tip. A 7,142 ton cargo vessel *SS Fort Stikine* from England carrying approximately two million pounds worth of assorted goods, including gold bars, sulphur, resin, oil, and 8,700 bales of raw cotton, mysteriously caught fire when it was anchored at Victoria Dock off the port city. Twin blasts

occurred that killed over 1,000 and left 3,000 injured. This explosion was so intense that old timers recall gold pieces falling from the sky and landing in their homes and terraces, making them rich overnight! A shred of the propeller from this ship landed on a section of St Xavier's Boys High School in Dhobi Talao, and can still be seen on the campus.

G
for
GATEWAY OF INDIA

THE GATEWAY OF INDIA and Victoria Terminus (now Chhatrapati Shivaji Maharaj Terminus) are two of the most iconic and photographed landmarks of the city. But did you know that the grand Gateway of India built to welcome seafaring passengers to India was originally made from Plaster of Paris (PoP)?

The Gateway was built to commemorate the visit of King George V and Queen Mary to India in December 1911. In fact, before this, an iron shed in the shape of a Mongol tent stood at the pier. Following the news that the royal couple and their delegation had to disembark via steamship in Bombay en route to the Delhi Durbar, a temporary structure was created using PoP after dismantling the iron shed. The dome-shaped structure was surrounded by a specially constructed amphitheatre where Bombay's powerful and famous citizens and the British rulers greeted the King and Queen of England.

After the royal couple's departure to England in 1912, it was decided to build a permanent structure to record this historic visit. The citizens of Bombay as well as the government contributed towards its funding. It was modelled by Scottish architect George Wittet as a cross between the Arc de Triomphe in Paris, a Moorish mansion and sixteenth century Gujarati architecture. One of the most respected architects for the Bombay government at the time, Wittet had also monitored the plan for the temporary structure. Yellow basalt stone from Kharodi in Thane and pierced stone panels from Gwalior were used to build the Gateway. Its main arch reaches a maximum height of eighty-three feet. When India gained Independence, the last British troops, belonging to the 1st Battalion, Somerset Light Infantry left the nation's shores in February 1948 from the Gateway. Bombay's residents lined the Apollo Bunder pier as they waved goodbye to the final remainder of colonialism.

The next time you stroll by the Arabian Sea-facing landmark, crane your neck a little to read the text etched on the main façade. It's the perfect way to relive those historic dates that are timeless reminders of how this monument is connected to the city.

Where: Apollo Bunder, Opposite Taj Mahal Hotel and Towers, Colaba

---

G *for* Gymkhanas: Where sport and leisure mixed

British residents in Bombay introduced clubs, known as gymkhanas where the rich and famous of the city (entry was open to only white people in the early days) relaxed, interacted with fellow club members, played sport—primarily cricket, rugby and indoor sports. Some of the popular ones that remain include Bombay Gymkhana, Wodehouse Gymkhana and Willingdon Gymkhana.

The Bombay Gymkhana, established in 1875, was the venue for the first ever cricket Test played in Bombay in 1933. Douglas Jardine captained the touring English side, while India was led by C.K. Nayudu. India lost by nine wickets, but Lala Amarnath scored a century on debut.

H
for
HORNBILL HOUSE

NONE OF US alive would've seen William. The Great Pied Hornbill flew into the office of the Bombay Natural History Society in its initial years, and made the secretary's office his home, living behind his chair. Today's Hornbill House that houses the offices of the Bombay Natural History (BNHS), is named after him. It is one of Asia's largest and oldest wildlife NGOs to preserve the natural heritage of the Indian Subcontinent. Back in 1883, a group of concerned citizens, comprising six Englishmen and two Indians, came together when they felt the need to discuss and record developments about the region's rich flora and fauna. Their office shifted address many times, yet the research continued in full swing. With time, BNHS's archives became a treasure chest for wildlife conservation. After Independence, the state government decided to fund the Society's rich collections of exhibits, archives and publications. When the present-day building for BNHS was finally opened in 1965, William the Great Hornbill was memorialised forever.

Where: Opposite Lion Gate, Shahid Bhagat Singh Marg, Fort

COOL FACT › INDIA'S BIRD MAN

The most respected name connected with BNHS's legacy is the late Dr Salim Ali also known as 'The Bird Man of India'. His findings in avian studies and books are respected and read across the world. As a ten-year-old, he shot a sparrow with a yellow streak below its neck with an air gun gifted to him by his uncle.

Unable to identify the bird, his uncle suggested that young Ali visit BNHS, where he was introduced to W.S. Millard, its honorary secretary. Millard helped him identify the bird—a Yellow-Throated Sparrow. He showed him the collection of stuffed birds. And that's how he got hooked on ornithology (the study of birds). Apart from documenting India's bird population for decades, he played a critical role in helping set up the Bharatpur Bird Sanctuary and the Ranganathittu Bird Sanctuary. He also saved the Silent Valley National Park in Kerala.

I
for
IRANI CAFÉS

SORRY
NO FIGHTING
NO CREDIT
NO BEEF
NO SPITTING
NO BARGAINING
NO COMBING
NO OUTSIDE FOOD
NO CHANGE
NO CHEATING
NO LEG ON CHAIR
NO ADD. ENQUIRY
NO TALKING LOUD
NO SITTING LONG
NO GAMBLING
NO LIQUOR
NO SMOKING

NO SITTING LONG * No talking loud * No gum under table * No leg on chair * No free advice.

Where in Mumbai will you come across such delightfully quirky instructions? You are most likely to spot these signboards in some of the city's Irani cafés. The Irani café emerged in the mid-nineteenth century, and continues to be run by members of the Parsi and Iranian Zoroastrian communities. These spaces almost always occupy the corners of buildings because Hindus believed it inauspicious to purchase such properties. They stand as silent testimony of the enterprise and hard work of these migrants in cosmopolitan Mumbai. Be it freshly baked brun, crispy chicken puffs or mutton sandwiches slathered with butter, the items on their sparse menus are unlike anything you will find in other city eateries. Over time, many cafés expanded to include restaurant-type fare, such as berry pulao, dhansak, lagan nu custard and patra ni macchi.

Some like Kyani (1904), Sassanian (1913) and B. Merwan and Co. (1914) remain unfazed and untouched by the lure of commercialisation, and have stuck to their original menus. These cafés stand out for their no-nonsense service, limited working hours, vintage decor and decrepit charm, apart from the delicious homely food. Yet, in today's times, these guardians of a unique culinary tradition are fighting for survival due to real estate sharks and redevelopment, sky-high rents and lack of support to continue, since most establishments are family-run.

Where: Kyani, Dhobi Talao; Koolar & Co., King's Circle; B. Merwan and Co., near Grant Road station; Sassanian, Dhobi Talao; Café Dela Paix, Girgaum; Britannia & Co., Ballard Estate; Café Colony and Stores, Dadar TT Circle; Café Military, Fort; Regal Restaurant & Bakery, Byculla East; Café Excelsior, near Chhatrapati Shivaji Maharaj Terminus; Ideal Corner, Fort; Yazdani Restaurant & Bakery, near Horniman Circle

COOL FACT › THE BRITISH ROYAL FAMILY FAN

In September 2019, Mumbai lost one of its most iconic characters, Boman Kohinoor, who was the owner of Britannia & Co. Restaurant and Stores in Ballard Estate. The ninety-seven-year-old had earned global fame after he met the Prince and Princess of Wales, William and Kate, on their official visit to India in 2016. The nonagenarian believed he was 'India's biggest fan of the British Royal Family', and would often regale patrons by pointing them towards photographs of the late Queen Elizabeth II and other royals that are proudly displayed on the walls of the slightly decrepit restaurant-café. The café, known for its berry pulao, remains a local attraction, especially among foreign tourists.

J
for
J.J. SCHOOL OF ART

'A MENACE'—This is how a colleague of John Lockwood Kipling, architectural sculptor and teacher at Sir J.J. School of Art, and father of Nobel laureate Rudyard Kipling, described his young son who was born on campus on December 30, 1865. The little menace who spent his early childhood on campus went on to write several literary classics including *The Jungle Book.*

In the mid-1800s, Sir Jamsetjee Jeejeebhoy approached the Bombay Government for land to build a school of art. The prestigious educational institution, Asia's oldest, was named after this eminent philanthropist, entrepreneur and visionary. The area where today's J.J. School of Art is located was a 'heavily wooded area' outside the Fort walls. After Sir J.J.'s petition was sanctioned, his generous contribution of Rs one lakh ensured work began in full swing. While the institution was founded in March 1857, the first structure—the School of Art—was established in 1874 with designs by G.T. Molecey. The School of Architecture was built by George Wittet, who designed the Gateway of India and The Prince of Wales Museum (today's Chhatrapati Shivaji Maharaj Vastu Sangrahalaya). Sadly, Sir Jeejeebhoy passed away in 1859, and was unable to see his vision become a reality. Early lectures were held at Elphinstone College before the first structures came up. In fact, some classes were also held in shamianas on site! Baby Rudyard, in all probability, was born in a tent somewhere on campus. The Department of Architecture came later (1913), as did the Institute of Applied Art (1935).

Kipling senior, John Griffiths and Wilkins Terry were some of the leading visionaries who laid the foundation of art studies here. Kipling's students played a key role by introducing beautiful ornamentation in the form of flora and fauna (mongoose, rat, peacock, rabbit and monkey in lifelike form) most notably seen at Victoria Terminus (today's Chhatrapati Shivaji Maharaj Terminus), Municipal Corporation building and Bombay University complex buildings in Fort, as well as the fountain inside Crawford Market. Griffiths, who was Kipling's friend, documented the paintings of Ajanta Caves that changed the course of art research in India. Terry was a pioneer in fine arts studies and revolutionised the use of pottery kilns that later became popular in Europe. He invented a style of ceramics known as Bombay Pottery. Examples of such works are on display at Dr Bhau Daji Lad Museum in Byculla. The present school of Architecture was originally designed by George Wittet in 1910 as Sir George Clarke Studios and Laboratories for developing ceramics on campus. It was given to the Department of Architecture a few years later.

This prestigious institute has produced some of India's biggest names in art, including M.V. Dhurandhar, Vasudeo Gaitonde, Akbar Padamsee, Tyeb Mehta and Prabhakar Kolte, as well as contemporary artists like Bose Krishnamachari, Atul Dodiya, Jitish Kallat and Shilpa Gupta. Notable alumni from the School of Architecture include names like Achyut Kanvinde and Balkrishna Doshi.

It's not just the buildings on site; old timers swear that if you walk around its campus, you will spot peepal and banyan trees that are as old as its structures!

Where: Dr D.N. Road

J *for* **Jehangir Art Gallery: Canvas for the city**

Ever wondered which is one of the most coveted spaces where Mumbai's artists—famous and new talent—would prefer to display their works? The outright response, almost always, would be Jehangir Art Gallery that was established in 1952 at Kala Ghoda. Designed by Durga Bajpai, this gallery remains one of Mumbai's earliest and most prominent concrete structures that emerged in post-Independence India. The generosity of Parsi philanthropist Sir Cowasji Jehangir, Second Baronet, ensured the city got a prestigious landmark that would become a hub to showcase modern Indian art across styles and schools.

K
for
KALA GHODA

BEFORE 2017, the art district of Kala Ghoda continued to be referred to by this generic name though there was no black horse (kala ghoda) in sight. What were the origins of Kala Ghoda? To answer this, we need to travel back to 1879. The original equestrian statue was a tribute to Edward VII, then Prince of Wales, and later King of England, seated on a black horse. The statue, a gift to the city by philanthropist Sir Albert Sassoon, was inaugurated in 1879 on a traffic island in the heart of this neighbourhood that lay along the southern edge of the now-gone Fort walls. The sculpture was designed by Sir Joseph Boehm and cost Rs 12,500. The 12 foot-9-inch high bronze statue's presence gave the area its name. Post Independence, nationalist feelings grew stronger, and it was felt that colonial reminders of the British Raj should not occupy vantage spots in the city. So in 1965, Kala Ghoda was moved to an oval garden inside Rani Baug (Veermata Jijabai Bhonsle Udyan) in Byculla. Statues of other English administrators and rulers in the city centre were shifted to the lawns of the Dr Bhau Daji Lad City Museum nearby.

The statue was gone but people continued to refer to the area as 'Kala Ghoda'. Over time, it emerged as a hub for art, education and culture, surrounded by the Chhatrapati Shivaji Maharaj Vastu Sangrahalaya (formerly Prince of Wales Museum), Jehangir Art Gallery, Elphinstone College, Max Mueller Bhavan as well as restaurants and indie shopping boutiques. By the early 2000s, the annual Kala Ghoda Festival became the city's most popular cultural gathering. Its stakeholders, the Kala Ghoda Association commissioned, a new Kala Ghoda to grace the area, and so finally, after five decades, in January 2017, the precinct got back its black horse but without King Edward VII as

its rider at a spot near where the original statue stood. Called 'The Spirit of Kala Ghoda', the installation was designed by Alfaz Miller and sculpted by Shreehari Bhosle. Thus, it brought back a visual connection with the area that was missing ever since King Edward and his equally famous horse moved to Byculla.

Where: Mahatma Gandhi Road, Fort

K *for* Khotachiwadi: East Indian legacy

Deep in the heart of chaotic Girgaum, Khotachiwadi is an oasis of calm stuck in a time warp. This small cluster of quaint one- and two-storeyed nineteenth century bungalows influenced by Portuguese and vernacular architecture remains one of the last original settlements of the East Indians in the island city. The area was originally owned by a Hindu khot (lessee of land; revenue collector) who sold it to his East Indian acquaintances. These families went on to build homes where you can still spot balconies decorated with wrought iron and stained glass motifs. Its heritage value is immense due to its status in its original avatar, and to the fact that it has managed to hold off redevelopment until now. Fashion designer James Ferreira, an East Indian resident of Khotachiwadi, is at the forefront of the movement to protect this neighbourhood. He hosts weekend bazaars in his bungalow to support independent platforms. The opening of 47-A Design Gallery in 2022 in a restored home in this area has also drawn public attention and is a shot in the arm for the measures to protect this important piece of local urban heritage.

❁ L ❁

for

LADY JAMSETJEE ROAD

TODAY, THE MAHIM CAUSEWAY might be the lesser preferred route to head from Mahim to Bandra or vice versa because of the Bandra-Worli Sea Link. However, this important road dates back to the 1840s, and has a fascinating backstory that led to its construction. Mahim and Bandra at the time were situated on two islands, and citizens had to use boats to commute. Lady Jamsetjee Road, or L.J. Road, is named after Avabai or Lady Jamsetjee, wife of Parsi industrialist-philanthropist and patron, Sir Jamsetjee Jeejeebhoy.

There are two accounts of how this road was built. According to the first one, of the wealthy businessman's children, the three sons were healthy, but the daughters did not survive beyond the age of two or three. The daughter of his Goan Catholic friend, Sir Roger de Faria, suggested making a vow to the Lady of the Mount (Mount Mary's Basilica in Bandra located on the Salsette Island). In 1834, a girl, Pirojbai, was born to the Jeejeebhoys. As she grew, the vow was renewed annually till she turned seven. Lady Jamsetjee vowed to make it easier for devotees to visit the Mount.

The second episode records that in 1841, a terrible boat tragedy occurred on the government-run ferry service between Mahim and Bandra where 15-20 boats capsized, causing a huge loss of lives and livestock. It shocked Bombay's prominent citizens, including the Jeejeebhoys. In fact, according to local history records, Sir Jamsetjee, by that time, was already in talks with the government to construct this permanent road, as a fulfilment of Avabai's vow. The tragedy made him more determined to realise this project so people could avoid using the sea route. By 1843, work began thanks to Sir Jamsetjee's cheque of Rs one lakh that was part payment. In 1845, the causeway was opened to the public; the road from the entry point in Bandra all the way to the Basilica was extended in 1854 by joint funding from Sir Jeejeebhoy and the government.

Soon enough, the suburb's prominence grew with the railway line entering Bandra (1888) and the rest of Salsette Island. The next time you use Mahim Causeway, whisper a little 'thank you' to the Jeejeebhoys, who ensured the safety of citizens by connecting the two islands by land.

Where: Mahim West

M
for
METRO CINEMA

MUMBAI'S LOVE AFFAIR with the movies dates back to 1896 with the first screening held by the Lumière brothers. Since then, filmmaking and film-viewing have had a happy co-existence. While multiplexes have been the popular choice for the past few decades, in the early days, luxurious single-screen cinema halls were a huge draw. The 1930s witnessed the rise of these cinemas, built in the Art Deco style, with its bold, geometric designs and progressive patterns to reflect a changing world. Metro, Regal, Eros, Liberty, Edward, New Empire and New Excelsior were some of the notable cinemas in Bombay that adopted this style.

Metro was designed by theatre architect Thomas W. Lamb (who assigned the task to Bombay architect D.W. Ditchburn). Opened in 1938, it was originally run by Metro-Goldwyn-Mayer (MGM) who acquired it for a 999-year lease. The single-screen cinema was built on a plot that was earlier used for the stables of the Auxiliary Forces (India)! Initially, it only screened movies by MGM but after its ownership changed to Indian hands, it became a favourite for red-carpet Hindi film premiers. The first Filmfare Awards were held here in 1954. Its marble foyer and staircases, and murals by students of Sir J.J. School of Art were the highlights of Metro. It was converted into a multiplex in 2006. Thankfully, after it became a six-screen multiplex, some elements of its Art Deco architecture, including its trademark signage and interiors, were retained. Metro's facelift ensured its longevity but others like New Excelsior, New Empire and Aurora had to shut down. The survivors continue to wage a long battle to stay relevant, with the hope of a fairytale ending, just like in the movies.

Where: Dhobi Talao junction, Marine Lines

DID YOU KNOW?

UNESCO conferred on Mumbai the prestigious tag of Creative City of Film in 2019 for its Hindi film industry, known the world over as Bollywood. Nearly fifty per cent of all Indian films and TV shows are conceptualised and created here.

M *for* Mithi River: Salty waters

Each time the city witnesses a heavy downpour, all eyes are on the water levels of the tiny Mithi River that worms its way through some of the most congested parts of suburban Mumbai until it reaches Mahim Creek. But do you know the infamous river derives its name from the fact that the water is somewhat salty and not sweet (in Marathi, meeth translates to salt)? In the old days, at high tide, the sea water would rise high enough to enter into the very flow of this river as it crossed areas like Khar and Kalina (that were part of Salsette Island; today's suburban Mumbai) where its villages were partly covered with salt pans. It is said that the water of this river was so salty that the fishermen of Kalina, Sion and Dharavi Koliwada would catch fish that were typically found only in salt water.

❁ **N** ❁

for

NAVAL DOCKYARD

WHEN THE BRITISH EAST INDIA Company decided to shift their administrative hub from Surat to Bombay in the early 1700s, developing their maritime might along the natural harbour was a top priority. Lowjee (Lovji) Nusserwanjee, master shipbuilder from the Surat Shipyard, was invited by the Company to modernise the Bombay Naval Dockyard and build ships for the company's maritime force. The dockyard was established in 1735 and thus the building of ships commenced. The Bombay Dock, Asia's first dry dock to support a natural harbour, was commissioned in 1750. Nusserwanjee went on to craft fine ships of Malabar teak that were used even by the British Admiralty! The company was so impressed with this contribution that they rewarded him with the title of 'Wadia' (shipbuilder) which was later adopted as a surname by his descendants.

The Treaty of Nanking (1842) that ceded Hong Kong to the British, was signed on board HMS Cornwallis, which was also built at the Bombay Dockyard. Apart from ship repairs, new ships were also built here. Soon, it was the nucleus around which the city developed as a naval and shipping hub. Today, this high-security zone is responsible for the repair and refitting of Indian naval ships and submarines. City historian late Foy Nissen made an interesting observation: he called the dock frontage that lines Shahid Bhagat Singh Marg as 'the oldest surviving street line vista in Bombay' since it has remained untouched for over 200 years. While walking past this stretch, don't miss the bell clock tower and the weathervane that rises above the walls of this landmark. Both remain silent remnants of a bygone era and of Bombay's timeless association with the sea and shipbuilding.

Where: Shahid Bhagat Singh Marg, formerly Dockyard Road, Fort

COOL FACT › MUMBAI'S CONNECT WITH THE STAR-SPANGLED BANNER

American lawyer Francis Scott Key was on board the HMS Minden when he wrote 'The Star-Spangled Banner'. He was on a visit to Baltimore. The poem went on to become the national anthem of the United States of America. HMS Minden was the first ship from India to be commissioned by the Royal Navy. It was launched in 1810 from Duncan Dock in the Naval Dockyard, and was the first to be built outside the United Kingdom. A miniature model of this ship is on display at the heritage gallery at Mazagon Dock Shipbuilders Limited. It is based on drawings sourced from the original blueprint at the National Maritime Museum in the United Kingdom.

N *for* Noor Mohammadi Hotel: Chicken and celebrities

This nondescript eatery in the heart of Bhendi Bazaar has a connect with Bollywood actor Sanjay Dutt who regularly orders in from here. One day, he cooked a chicken dish in his home kitchen and sent it to the owners, who liked it so much that the dish is now part of their menu, and is served as Chicken Sanju Baba.

Celebrated artist M.F. Husain was a frequent visitor. During one such visit, Husain enjoyed his meal so much that he created an art work with his trademark rooster to show his gratitude. Customers can still spot this frame on one of its walls.

O
for
OVAL MAIDAN

LIKE CALCUTTA AND MADRAS, Bombay also had an Esplanade. Until the 1860s, this was a huge, undivided, open stretch of land that overlooked the Arabian Sea. The Esplanade offered a clear firing range for the British military that was positioned at vantage points along the long-gone Fort walls to be watchful for incoming enemies from the sea. Some soldiers who found the summers unbearable would pitch their canvas tents on the open ground.

When Arthur Crawford, the city's first Municipal Commissioner, decided to lay out avenues through the Esplanade, this space was divided into smaller enclosures that came to be known as maidans. There were four such partitions—Cooperage and Oval maidan towards the southern end near Colaba, and Azad and Cross maidans to the north.

With the Oval, the idea was to connect the Fort area with the western foreshore that overlooks the Arabian Sea near today's Churchgate railway terminus. Oval got its name from the shape it acquired after the Esplanade was partitioned. The twenty-two-acre space was popular among citizens who would enjoy sweeping views of the sea with the imposing University building complex, including the Rajabai Tower, and the High Court, lording over the maidan. Bands performed in the evenings; it was popular among British settlers who played cricket here. Interestingly, if you visit the green space today, you will notice that it is a favourite for aspiring cricketers. The maidan is home to 540 trees.

By the 1930s, after land was reclaimed from the sea as part of the Backbay Reclamation Scheme, plots were available on this maidan's western edge. These buildings were touted as Bombay's most modern residences, and remain a contrast to the British-inspired Victorian and Gothic landmarks that are on the other side of the Oval. This style spread to other parts of Bombay, including Marine Drive.

The next time you are near Churchgate, walk around the Oval to fully understand its historic character, from the nineteenth century Victorian Gothic public buildings on one side, to the Art Deco residences on the other. The Eros Cinema building near the northern edge of the maidan is the only commercial Art Deco building in this stretch.

Where: Maharshi Karve Marg and Karmaveer Bhaurao Marg, Churchgate

COOL FACT › HURRAH FOR PEOPLE POWER

The Art Deco buildings along with Oval maidan and the Victorian-Gothic Ensembles formed part of the city's third UNESCO World Heritage Site in 2018. It was the first time that local citizens' groups were directly associated with preparing a nomination. UNESCO lauded their effort of being at the forefront to protect these heritage landmarks spanning centuries. Today, these groups continue to create awareness with walks, discussions and dialogues.

P
for
PORT TRUST WAR MEMORIAL

DID YOU KNOW that in August 1914, 1,87,000 Indian troops set sail from Bombay's port to fight for Great Britain in World War I? Or that over twenty-two lakh tons of military supplies were shipped off to help these soldiers during this same war? We didn't know either, until we read facts at the Port Trust World War Memorial that stands at a major junction in Ballard Estate. This business and commercial district designed by Scotsman George Wittet, was named after J.A. Ballard, the first chairman of the Bombay Port Trust.

Located near the port and harbour, you can spot this sandstone memorial with its imposing lamp post from a distance. The landmark is one of the few remaining monuments to salute India's contribution in World War I. Once there, check out more amazing details that are etched on the brass plaques fixed along the base of this structure. We suggest you also take a closer look at the detailed carvings of winged lions. And, whisper a prayer for those brave Indian soldiers who laid down their lives for their British rulers.

Diagonally opposite this memorial is the Ballard Bunder Gate that was once referred to as the actual 'Gateway of India'. It led to Ballard Pier, where passenger ships as well as steamer vessels would dock. It is from this gate that its occupants would pass through to enter into the city. Passengers who had trains to board from the nearby Ballard Pier station to other parts of the Subcontinent would stay at the Grand or Regent Hotels located within the Estate until their train's departure.

Where: Near Britannia Restaurant, Shoorji Vallabhdas Road, Ballard Estate

---

P *for* Portuguese Church: The Correa-Husain partnership

Originally built by Portuguese Franciscans in the late 1500s, the Our Lady of Salvation Church in Dadar, popularly called Portuguese Church, has been rebuilt several times down the centuries. The present structure was redesigned in 1977 by celebrated architect Charles Correa as one of the earliest modern-styled churches in Mumbai. He approached the iconic artist M.F. Husain who created a stunning fresco design on glass on its roof depicting Christ's miracle of the two fish and five loaves of bread, his death and resurrection.

P *for* Prince Of Wales Museum: When it was a hospital ...

Did you know that the Prince of Wales Museum (renamed Chhatrapati Shivaji Maharaj Vastu Sangrahalaya [CMSVS] in 1998) was temporarily converted into a hospital when World War I broke out in 1914? At the time, the site, designed by George Wittet, was nearing completion. It was named The Lady Hardinge War Hospital, and treated wounded Indian soldiers who fought for the Crown in Africa and other battlegrounds. When the war ended in 1918, work resumed to complete the museum, and it was finally opened in 1922. Today, as a leading museum in India, it welcomes over a million visitors annually. It is home to one of the largest collections, including private collections by Sir Ratan Tata and the Natural History Gallery as well as international collaborations. In March 2019, the city got its first dedicated Children's Museum inside the CSMVS complex. In Novemeber 2022, the museum won the Award of Excellence, the highest honour at the UNESCO Asia-Pacific Awards for Cultural Heritage Conservation that took place in Bangkok.

P *for* Prithvi Theatre: Cradle of theatre in the suburbs

Named after Prithviraj Kapoor, doyen of the famous film and theatre family, Prithvi Theatre as a venue was inaugurated in November 1978 in honour of his life and work. The intimate space located in Juhu's Janki Kutir neighbourhood near Juhu Beach was the first venue planned as an amphitheatre to promote an informal, interactive connection between the actors and the audience. Today, the theatre is helmed by Prithviraj's grandson, Kunal Kapoor, eldest son of the late Shashi and Jennifer Kapoor.

Q
for
QUEEN'S NECKLACE

MARINE DRIVE, the nearly four-kilometre-long iconic sea-facing promenade, is commonly referred to as the 'Queen's Necklace'. When viewed at night from an elevated point any where along the stretch, the street lights resemble a string of pearls in a necklace. Marine Drive was previously called Kennedy Road, and an inscription near Girgaum Chowpatty states that work on Kennedy Sea-Face began on December 18, 1915 and was completed in 1920. The line-up was part of the Backbay Reclamation Scheme where land was reclaimed along the western shore of the Arabian Sea.

The remaining work that was under the Marine Drive Scheme extended all the way to the National Centre for Performing Arts, and it continued till the 1930s. Did you know that the Art Deco buildings that you can spot on this sea-facing promenade are part of the second largest display of this architectural style in the world, after Miami? These buildings were designed by Indian architects in this style that was a contrast to the British-influenced Gothic, Neoclassical and Victorian styles that were seen across most of the city landmarks at the time. These residential buildings boasted of well-ventilated balconies, striking geometric patterns and state-of-the-art facilities.

This style was used nearly two decades before India attained Independence. It forms part of the Victorian Gothic and Art Deco Ensembles that earned the city its most recent UNESCO World Heritage Site tag in 2018. This sea-facing promenade is one of the most photographed landmarks in Mumbai.

The next time you walk down the Queen's Necklace or are seated on the promenade, look closely at these first 'modern' planned buildings and remember why they are a special part of the city after all these decades.

Where: Netaji Subhash Chandra Bose Road

COOL FACT › A BADLY FIT IDEA

'A rather badly fitting set of false teeth to the city.'

Not everyone in the city was happy about the new sea-facing buildings. Claude Batley, leading British architect of Bombay and academician and head of the Architectural Department at Sir J.J. School of Art (1923-43), was one of the most vocal critics of the Marine Drive Scheme. He felt that the promenade was planned by the government in such a way that long blocks of uniformly designed buildings were given minimum exposure to the western seafront. Batley felt that these buildings were separated by narrow lanes and bylanes, thus robbing the chance of giving Bombay a more world-class character.

R
for
RANI BAUG

IN THE MID-1800s, Byculla in south-central Mumbai was a buzzing location, home to the rich and famous. This was also where many public welfare projects, including the Victoria Gardens, were set up. The Victoria Gardens were established in 1862 as the city's largest botanical gardens after being shifted from Sewri to Byculla. The gardens boast of diverse fauna from India and other parts of the world. The complex also houses a public zoo. Named after Queen Victoria, the complex was thrown open to the public in November 1862. The complex was later renamed as Veermata Jijabai Bhonsle Udyan after Chhatrapati Shivaji Maharaj's mother. Today, the gardens and the zoo are collectively called Rani Baug by most of Mumbai's citizens.

In the same complex, a museum was originally established in 1855 as the Government Central Economic Museum of the Bombay Presidency, thus becoming the first museum to open in the city. The building on the present site came up in 1872 as the Victoria and Albert Museum. In 1975, it was renamed after Dr Bhau Daji Lad, who was a key visionary and scholar. He raised public funds for the museum's construction. The museum opened a decade later as the city's first museum. If you're in Byculla, step inside to gaze at its rare collections, displays and objects sourced from across India. Don't miss the section of dioramas that explain how Bombay evolved from seven islands to its current form, and also miniatures showing people in period dress and their professions. After extensive restorations for five years, the museum reopened in January 2008. This effort earned it the UNESCO Asia-Pacific Award for Excellence in Conservation in 2005.

Rani Baug is also a protected area, and many citizen groups are doing their best to create awareness of its rich flora. To know more about this diversity, keep an eye out for the tree walks organised inside these gardens, where experts share fascinating information about this example of natural heritage in the heart of the city.

Where: Dr B.R. Ambedkar Road, near Byculla East railway station

R *for* Ranwar, Bandra: Village by the sea

One of the original villages of Bandra that exists to this day is worth walking through for its quaint character. Remnants of that earlier time will give you an idea of what life would have been like in a palm-fringed, fishing village in Bandora (today's Bandra). It was then part of Salsette Island, north of the seven islands of Bombay. Look out for its tiled roofs and stone facades, charming cottages with verandahs, as well as crucifixes and grottos at street junctions and corners. Barely 400 metres from here is the Church of St Andrew's, Bandra's oldest standing church that dates back to the 1700s. It has a 'Juliet Balcony' [that resembles the one from the Shakespearean classic, *Romeo and Juliet*], from where senior priests could attend mass while staying out of view of the congregation.

R *for* Racecourse: Canter from Byculla to Mahalaxmi

The racecourse was originally located in Byculla, and the races became a popular pastime for its residents. However as the area became more congested, living conditions and sanitation facilities came under pressure. Soon, its elite shifted to other parts of the city. The racecourse too moved to a plot in Mahalaxmi that was originally a low-lying swamp near today's Haji Ali that got flooded every monsoon. It had to be levelled to make it suitable for racing, and allow for the accompanying infrastructure like stables. The current site, designed under the direction of Major J.E. Hughes, was built in 1883. The design was based on the Flemington racecourse in Melbourne because Sir Cusrow N. Wadia—who donated land for the Mahalaxmi racecourse—wanted it to be a near replica of it. Known as the Royal Western India Turf Club, it hosts some of India's most prestigious races, including the Indian Derby and the Poonawalla Breeders Multimillion. Its grandstand is identified as a heritage structure.

R *for* **Royal Opera House: Let the stage reopen**

The Royal Opera House remains India's only surviving opera house. It was inaugurated in 1911 by King George V and was completed in 1916. It staged all the big theatre productions of the time. By 1925, the entire theatre was rented by British film equipment company Pathé for screening their films. Leading performers of the time like Bal Gandharva and Prithviraj Kapoor performed here. The site changed hands in 1952, when the Maharaja of Gondal, Shri Vikramsinhji, bought the Opera House. Over the years, stage productions stopped, and it fell into ruin. Finally, in 2010, the royal's son, the late Jyotendrasinhji, commissioned its restoration, and a century later after it was opened, it received the Award of Merit at the 2017 UNESCO Asia-Pacific Awards for Cultural Heritage Conservation.

S
for
SANJAY GANDHI NATIONAL PARK

ALONG WITH Table Mountain National Park in South Africa, Nairobi National Park in Kenya and Serra da Cantareira National Park in Brazil, Mumbai's Sanjay Gandhi National Park (SGNP) has the distinction of being among the few national parks that is within a city's municipal limits. Alternately referred to as the Borivali National Park, it is a verdant forest of approximately 104 square kilometres that lies in the northern outskirts of the metropolis. According to Dr Anish Andheria from the Wildlife Conservation Trust, SGNP is home to over 280 species of birds, nearly 1,400 species of plants, about 40 species of mammals, 61 species of reptiles, around 14 species of amphibians, 150 species of butterflies and an immeasurable array of other invertebrates.

The Tulsi and Vihar Lakes that supply water to the city were constructed within the park by the British in the second half of the 1800s. Several rivers like the Dahisar, Poisar and Mithi originate from the hills within this national park. This site is also a protected area, and is home to the Warli tribal community who worship Waghoba, which is an ancient tiger/leopard deity. In the heart of SGNP lie Kanheri Caves, a 2,000-year-old rock-cut site that was once inhabited by Buddhist monks. A popular spot for historians, naturalists and trekkers, its summit offers panoramic views of suburban Mumbai. In 2020, in a landmark development, the state government announced that 812 acres of Aarey Colony adjacent to SGNP will be a forest area, thus offering more space for the park's fauna. Yet, man-animal conflict continues to be a concern on the outskirts of the park due to illegal occupation of forest lands.

If you're keen to explore SGNP's flora and fauna as well as its caves and other discoveries, check out their annual calendar of events that includes awareness programmes, trails and treks for all age groups.

Where: Western Express Highway, Borivali East

COOL FACT › WILD WONDERS

- SGNP has one of the highest densities of leopards anywhere in the world.
- It is home to the world's smallest wild cat, the rusty-spotted cat.

S *for* Sassoon: Benevolence and business

Masina Hospital. Sassoon Dock. David Sassoon Library & Reading Hall—These are some of the surviving public landmarks that keep the legacy of Sir David Sassoon and his descendants alive. The visionary Baghdadi Jew, who arrived here from Persia in 1832, built his empire and left an imprint on the city. His palatial home in Byculla, called Sans Souci (French: No worries) later became Masina Hospital. Sassoon Dock was built as India's first wet dock in 1872 while the city's first library—David Sassoon Library & Reading Room was opened to the public in 1870. Along with Parsi industrialists and businessmen, the Sassoons were some of the most generous citizens who funded city public buildings, including the Prince of Wales (now Chhatrapati Shivaji Maharaj Vastu Sangrahalaya) and Victoria & Albert (now Dr Bhau Daji Lad) Museums, and the Gateway of India.

S *for* **Sewri Cemetery: Where the famous rest**

During Municipal Commissioner Arthur Crawford's reign (1865), he acquired land on the eastern front in Sewri for a large burial ground to cater to Bombay's European Christian population. Spread over forty acres of land, it is one of Asia's oldest and largest cemeteries with more than 20,000 graves. Since Independence, it is mostly used by Indian Christians. Once inside, you will see the graves of the city's founding fathers and famous Indians. While F.W. Stevens, who designed the Victoria Terminus building, has a simple grave, the Gateway's architect George Wittet's grave is just an entry in the cemetery's register since it is lost in the undergrowth, with no visible tombstone! Italian prisoners of war from World War II have a separate memorial within the cemetery. Actor 'Fearless' Nadia, artist F.N. Souza and poet-author Dom Moraes are all buried here.

S *for* **Sion: Entry point to Bombay**

On a conical hill in Sion on Salsette Island is a seventeenth-century fort built by the British forces since the area stood at an important connecting point between Salsette and Bombay. The fort acted as a vantage point in case enemies decided to attack the Bombay islands. Though it is now in ruins, historian Gillian Tindall's findings reveal that there was a time when it served as a 'pleasant spot for a Sunday picnic'.

T
for
THANA / THANE

FOR MANY OF US, when we mention Thane, what instantly comes to mind is that it was the final destination of Asia's first rail journey. Engineered by the Great Indian Peninsula Railway (GIPR, today's Central Railway), this historic, fifty-seven-minute-run was flagged off from Bori Bunder on April 16, 1853 to its terminus in Thana. On that day, senior officers of the GIPR raised a toast to Queen Victoria, hailing a new era in the Subcontinent's transport history.

However, Thane was a key trading port as far back as the post-Gupta period, when it was engaged in trade with local, regional and foreign lands. Its importance as a major coastal centre emerges again in a copperplate record dating to 1094, along with Chaul and Sopara (today's Nala Sopara). What is interesting is that as a maritime and commercial hub, Thane predates its illustrious neighbour, Bombay, which at the time was a marshy cluster of seven islands.

The region has been variously referred to as Sri Sthanaka, Thannah, Tana, and Thana in local records. The Masunda Lake, popularly known as Talao Pali, remains a prominent landmark. It is also one of Thane's last surviving lakes that were once commonly found here, lending it the title 'City of Lakes'. According to Thane historian Dr Fleur D'Souza, these lakes were stone tanks that were laid a thousand years ago by the ruling Shilahara dynasty.

Thane had a rollercoaster history with different rulers. It was handed over to the Portuguese in the mid-1500s and later changed hands with the Marathas and eventually fell into British control by the late 1700s. Throughout this time, it remained a busy port, trading in cloth, silks, leather, salt, coconuts and oil. After the railway line reached Thane, it offered new opportunities for its residents to explore in Bombay, which by then had risen to be the seat of commerce in West India.

Thanks to its trading ties from ancient times, Thane has always welcomed people of all faiths. Hindus, Muslims, Jews, Parsis and Christians have lived here, and continue to do so till date. Post Independence, Thane became independent India's first industrial zone. If you're in Thane, catch a glimpse of the sluggishly flowing Thane Creek that was once the centre of the region's historic seafaring ties with the world, and the eighteenth-century fort that now houses the Central Jail. Next, head to Masunda Lake, to see the Kopineshwar Temple. Built in 1760, it is home to the patron God of Thana and also houses one of the biggest Shiva Lingas in Maharashtra.

Where: Thane, Thane District, Maharashtra

COOL FACT › RETREAT FOR BOMBAYITES

Early twentieth century town planner Patrick Geddes envisioned Thane as a beautiful destination for Bombayites for leisurely getaways, rather than a dormitory town that emptied daily to the island city. His proposal suggested beautifying Masunda Tank (Lake), planting trees and even organising a grand Diwali celebration to promote community living. Many municipal authorities at the time disagreed with his ideas.

COOL FACT › GREEN COASTAL GUARDIANS

In May 2018, the Maharashtra government formally recognised the Thane Creek Flamingo Sanctuary as a protected area. It spreads across 1.690 hectares, and includes parts of suburban Mumbai. The sanctuary is home to over 12 species of mangroves and mangrove associates, approximately 167 species of birds including lakhs of flamingos that throng the area, 45 fish species and 50-plus butterfly species. Conservationists face a constant battle to protect this precious green cover lying in between the urban centres of

Thane city, Navi Mumbai and suburban Mumbai from commercial interests and infrastructure projects that threaten this wetland treasure. In August 2022, the sanctuary was designated a Ramsar site—a wetland of significant global importance. It is the first wetland in India with this honour and that too, within an urban metropolis, the Mumbai Metropolitan Region (MMR).

U
for
UNIVERSITY BUILDINGS

TWO OF BOMBAY'S most famous citizens in the 1800s—Sir Cowasjee Jehangir and Premchand Roychand—played a leading role in setting up the University Convocation Hall, the University Library and the Rajabai Tower that came to be known as the University buildings in Fort. Both were wealthy philanthropists who made generous contributions towards this seat of education. Bombay University was set up in 1857 but this complex was completed by 1880, when the Rajabai Tower became operational. Until then, lectures were held at the nearby Elphinstone College while University examinations were conducted in the Town Hall at the Asiatic Society.

Work on this site that faces Oval Maidan began in 1868 based on plans by George Gilbert Scott in the Victorian Gothic style. Traces of Venetian Gothic style can also be spotted here. Scott, who previously designed London's St Pancras Railway Station, never visited the city! He and his team ensured that the best minds from the United Kingdom worked with skilled Indian artisans and craftsmen, using locally sourced materials. The centerpiece of these grand buildings is the 280-feet-high Rajabai Clock Tower, which for a while was Bombay's tallest structure. Roychand, the first Indian broker who could read and write in English, profited from the stock market, and donated some of his surplus funds to build the Clock Tower, naming it in memory of his mother, Rajabai. Climbing up the library's grand central staircase might just transport you to Hogwarts School of Witchcraft and Wizardry. Leading upstairs, there are more sights to wow you, in the form of carved heads of literary greats like Homer and Shakespeare. Students from Sir J.J. School of Art helped execute these plans. Along with its second campus in suburban Kalina, the University's library boasts of over eight lakh titles as well as handwritten and palm leaf manuscripts.

The Sir Cowasjee Jehangir Hall, named after the benevolent businessman, has a circular rose window with stunning stained glass work that represents the zodiac signs as well as the twelve months of the year.

When you next pass by these buildings, slow down to gaze at the stunning designs and soak in the historic connections. And remember what a wonderful reminder it is of the city's generous spirit towards education. This cluster also forms the cove of the Victorian Gothic and Art Deco Ensembles that became Mumbai's third UNESCO World Heritage Site in 2018.

The refurbishment of Rajabai Clock Tower and University Library Building inside this complex took place in two phases—Phase 1 (2012-15) and Phase 2 (2018-21).

Where: Maharshi Karve Marg, opposite Oval Maidan, Fort

COOL FACT › WHO WAS 'READYMONEY'?

The wealthy Parsi, Sir Cowasjee Jehangir was bestowed with the title 'Readymoney' by the British for his generosity. Apart from funding the University's convocation hall, he also offered grants towards the building of Bombay's first college, Elphinstone College, besides a water fountain inside St Thomas Cathedral as well as many others across the city, the Bombay Gymkhana, an ophthalmic hospital and a museum. He was knighted as well as conferred with the title of Baronet by the British Crown.

V
for
VICTORIA TERMINUS

YOU MAY HAVE walked the corridors of Victoria Terminus (renamed Chhatrapati Shivaji Maharaj Terminus in 1996) hundreds of times. But have you looked upwards and at its walls and ceilings to check out the dazzling display of art, including floral patterns, peacocks, cobras, rats, owls, crocodiles, monkeys and gargoyles that are etched across its façades, arches and pillars?

These details, along with those on every corner, corridor and ceiling of this railway terminus, were actually hand-drawn by its architect, Frederick William Stevens. Such was his dedication to give the city a world-class landmark. After VT, he went on to build several others, including the Bombay Municipal Corporation building; Bombay Baroda and Central India Railway (today's Western Railway headquarters) at Churchgate with his son, Charles; Royal Alfred Sailors' Home (today's Maharashtra State Police Headquarters); and the Army and Navy Building.

When Asia's first railway was flagged off from Bori Bunder to Thana (today's Thane) on April 16, 1853, a public holiday was declared. Both Indians and British people lined the thirty-four-kilometre route to wave as the three locomotives, and fourteen coaches lugged 400 ticketed passengers on-board. However, Bori Bunder was just a temporary station not too far away from present-day VT.

With Bombay's rapid growth as a commercial city, and the need for better transport to connect it with the rest of the Subcontinent, the government and directors of the Great Indian Peninsula Railway (GIPR) wanted to build a permanent terminus to cater to passengers and its own staff in the same complex. Stevens, an employee of the Public Works Department, was selected by GIPR after they could not find a candidate in-house or from England. Work on the terminus began in 1878 and took a decade to complete. The mammoth project cost Rs 16,35,562 for the offices, while the station itself cost Rs 10,40,248. On Queen Victoria's Jubilee Day in 1887, it was named after the Empress of India.

Though planned in the Victorian Gothic style, Stevens' blueprint was a grand association between British architects, ably supported by Indian associates like Rao Saheb Sitaram Khanderao Vaidya and Mahderao Janardhan, and skilled local craftsmen. Staff and students of the Sir J.J. School of Art crafted elements within the building, and created models that were then executed by Indian craftsmen. Stevens's plan had wide, shaded verandahs to protect the occupants of the structure from heat and heavy rainfall. When the terminus was listed as a UNESCO World Heritage Site in 2004, this unique Indianised influence on the Gothic style came in for special mention.

Over 130 years later, with daily traffic of 663 locals (up and down), 102 mail/ express/passenger trains (up and down) and nearly five lakh commuters using its services, it continues to realise the role that Stevens and GIPR had envisioned for this historic landmark.

Where: Dr D.N. Road

COOL FACT › STARS AND STATUES

At the gate leading to the office blocks that face Dr D.N. Road, seated statues of the tiger and lion (representing India and Great Britain, respectively) welcome visitors. Along the façade of the building, there are eleven portrait roundels of its directors, including two Indians—Sir Jamsetjee Jeejeebhoy and Jagannath 'Nana' Sunkersett. A must-see is the Star Chamber, where you need to crane your neck to gaze at the glittering stars on the ceiling of the main booking office area. The most remarkable sight is at the terminus' highest point—the statue of a woman holding a lit torch and a wheel to symbolise progress.

COOL FACT › STEVENS IN SEWRI

F.W. Stevens passed away in 1900, while he was midway through overseeing plans for the Chartered Bank of India, Australia and China in Bombay. He was buried at the Sewri Christian Cemetery. His descendants still visit the grave of the great architect who gave the city a new style of architecture for its public buildings.

W
for
WANKHEDE STADIUM

MUMBAI LIVES and breathes cricket, and perhaps the biggest venue where this passion is visible, apart from its maidans, is the Wankhede Stadium. The stadium, one of India's largest, was named after S.K. Wankhede, the then president of the Mumbai Cricket Association. It was designed by Shashi Prabhu in record time to host the fifth and final India versus West Indies Test in January 1975, which decided the series in the visitors' favour (3-2). Interestingly, the stadium was built because of a dispute with the Cricket Club of India (CCI) over seats. Although the Brabourne Stadium housed the CCI, Test matches were allotted to the Mumbai Cricket Association.

The stadium underwent extensive renovation—overseen by Prabhu along with P.K. Das—and was ready in time for the 2011 One Day International World Cup. It hosted the final, where India famously defeated Sri Lanka to win the World Cup for the second time in history. Post the upgrade, the stadium's capacity was reduced from 45,000 to approximately 33,000. Wankhede has stands named after some of the city's most famous cricketers like Vijay Merchant, Sunil Gavaskar, Dilip Vengsarkar and Sachin Tendulkar.

Where: D Road, Churchgate

COOL FACT › VISHY, THE SPORTING CAPTAIN

It was at the Wankhede that India's sporting captain Gundappa Viswanath recalled Bob Taylor after he was adjudged caught behind by Syed Kirmani off Kapil Dev. India went on to lose the 1980 Test match but won countless hearts with his act of sportsmanship.

COOL FACT › KISS THE CRICKETER

Abbas Ali Baig is famously known as the cricketer who was kissed on the field by an admirer, at Brabourne Stadium in 1959-60, but India batsman Brijesh Patel too was in for a peck from a woman fan when he reached his half century in the second innings of the 1974-75 Wankhede Test.

W *for* Wellington Fountain: The Duke and the city

This functional ornamental fountain was built towards the entrance to Colaba in 1865, pre-dating Flora Fountain, in memory of the Duke of Wellington, Arthur Wellesley. He considered himself to be a loyal servant of the Crown, and so gave himself the title of 'nimmukwalla' for having eaten the King's salt! He had visited the city in 1801 and 1804. Over a century later, the city's oldest water fountain fell into neglect. It was eventually restored, for which it received an Honourable Mention at the 2017 UNESCO Asia-Pacific Awards for Cultural Heritage Conservation.

W *for* Worli: Shaping a city

One of the seven islands that comprised Bombay, Worli was a rocky isle. Like Sion on the eastern side, it became connected to the Bombay island when a causeway was completed by 1784. It was named Hornby Vellard (vallado is a local corruption of the Portuguese word for embankment) after Governor William Hornby, who was responsible for linking this island with the main island of Bombay and thus improving north-south connectivity. It remains one of the most historic (and earliest) milestones connected with shaping the city from seven islands into one land mass. Worli is also home to one of the oldest Koliwadas—a fishing village of the Kolis who remain one of the city's earliest inhabitants.

X

for

ST XAVIER'S BOYS HIGH SCHOOL, DHOBI TALAO

MANY OF US would have marvelled at the life-like displays in the Natural History section inside the Chhatrapati Shivaji Maharaj Vastu Sangrahalaya (CSMVS, formerly Prince of Wales Museum). But guess what? About two kilometres away, at St Xavier's High School (Boys), a similar collection exists, due to the efforts of Brother Antonio Navarro (1903-87), who was posted at the school for forty-six years.

Brother Navarro arrived in India in 1931, and when he was at St. Xavier's College, Father Gonzalo Palacios, a known naturalist, arranged for him to learn taxidermy at the Bombay Natural History Society (BNHS). After he moved to St Xavier's High School nearby, he almost single-handedly created and added these specimens to his dream project from 1945 until his death. He began his research in Karjat-Talegaon in the Khandala belt of the Western Ghats. Studying birds was his favourite activity, and after five years, he had documented 250 bird species. Later, he shifted to the Konkan coast, from Virar to Alibaug, including Vaitarna, Bassein and Revdanda. He worked closely with iconic ornithologist Dr Salim Ali.

Nearly 3,000 specimens are on display inside its Natural History Museum. It is possibly the only school in West India to boast of such a collection. Only CSMVS has a better and bigger collection in Mumbai. This section has been created within the school's corridors and is spread across four floors. Specimens of bird, animal and marine life are arranged and catalogued, stored and displayed in wood and glass enclosures.

You can spot displays of the Royal Bengal Tiger, Sloth Bear, Giant Black Turtle, Indian Pangolin, Mountain Goat, Gorilla, and even Wallaby and Black Swan, that were shipped from Australia. There are also butterflies, birds, and seventy-five varieties of bats, as well as reptiles and amphibians. The informative background displays were painted by P.V. Joshi, who accompanied Brother Navarro on several expeditions. The BNHS helps maintain this museum.

Where: St Xavier's High School, Lokmanya Tilak Marg, Dhobi Talao

COOL FACT › BABBLERS AND OTHER BIRD CALLS

Brother Navarro started recording bird calls in the forests of Khandala. Dumetia Hyperythra Navarroi (Navarro's White-Throated Babbler) named after Brother Navarro was a rare species that he discovered there in 1958. He helped BNHS with ornithological and other research for three decades. He even anchored a programme about birds on All India Radio. In 1977, the BBC announced an international competition for bird calls. Brother Navarro's excerpts from his collection won him the first prize!

Y

for

YACHT CLUB

THE ARABIAN SEA has been a muse to Bombay's citizens, as well as to artists, explorers and photographers. When the British arrived here, they looked for pastimes that would remind them of home. Sailing was an outdoor activity that soon became a passion.

With this intent, they set up the Bombay Yacht Club (BYC) in 1846, and thirty years later, thanks to the patronage of Queen Victoria, it came to be called Royal Bombay Yacht Club (RBYC). RBYC had two buildings—the clubhouse and the Annexe or Residential Chambers. Both were designed by famous city architect, John Adams. Adams built at least twenty-five buildings in Bombay, including landmarks like Wilson College, Cathedral and John Connon School, and the Mumbai Police Headquarters opposite Crawford Market.

The club building was constructed in 1881; it currently houses the offices of the Bhabha Atomic Research Centre (BARC) whereas the Annexe/ Residential Chambers is now the RBYC that was constructed in 1896-98. RBYC's design was overseen by none other than F.W. Stevens, the architect of the Victoria Terminus and Bombay Municipal Corporation buildings, and later, by Stevens's son, Charles. The club was fitted with lifts, electric lights, fire services, and different kinds of amenities of the time. It boasted of quite a few eminent visitors after it opened, including HRH Prince Arthur and American yachting enthusiast William Vanderbilt. After the visit of King George V and Queen Mary to India via Bombay in 1911, interest in yachting and sailing increased.

Post Independence, after the club building came under BARC, activities of both structures were merged into the Residential Chambers that is now referred to as the RBYC building. Apart from sailing facilities, a bar, billiards room, salon, restaurant, gymnasium, library, and the ballrooms. are on the lower two levels, while the top floors are for residential purposes.

Indians were offered membership only in the late 1950s. By the 1960s, RBYC introduced new races, and many of its members owned some of the most modern boats of the time. Today, it is one of the city's oldest surviving and most prestigious members-only clubs. If you step inside, the interiors will give you an idea of what life was like for the representatives of the Crown.

The Residential Chambers of the club underwent a restoration for which it received an Award of Merit at the 2013 UNESCO Asia-Pacific Awards for Cultural Heritage Conservation.

Where: Chhatrapati Shivaji Maharaj Marg, near Gateway of India, Apollo Bunder

COOL FACT › NO ROOM FOR MISBEHAVIOUR

Bernard Law Montgomery, 1st Viscount Montgomery of Alamein and decorated British field marshal and a brave Allied commander in World War II, was once reported for 'ungentlemanly behaviour' at the bar in this club. The letter from the secretary of the club added that his act had caused great annoyance to its members.

Z
for
ZAVERI BAZAAR

ZAVERI BAZAAR STARTED in 1864 in a tin shelter set up by a jeweller called Bhimji Zaveri who dared to dream big and take risks. He decided to name his venture after his son, Tribhovandas, who then went on to expand it by opening new showrooms. Since then, there has been no looking back for the iconic 'TBZ' brand. Today, fifth-generation family member Binaisha Zaveri is proud of her lineage, sharing that it was a natural calling for her forefathers to set up one of India's most recognisable jewellery businesses.

Soon, the store became one of the landmark buildings in a congested bazaar in Kalbadevi, and the family surname, 'Zaveri', got instantly linked with the area because of its popularity and impact on the jewellery market across India. As the family business expanded, branches opened beyond their Opera House address. By then, other jewellery traders also decided to set up shop here, as it became the heart of Mumbai's gold, silver and diamond trade.

Back in the day, because it was the main hub for buying bullion due to the number of bullion traders in the vicinity, gold prices set here often acted as the benchmark for prices in the rest of the country. The TBZ brand had many firsts to their name, such as being the first in India to offer lifetime buyback on gold and diamond jewellery. In the 1990s, they were the first to offer lightweight jewellery in India.

Today, if you head into the congested Opera House neighbourhood, you are sure to spot multiple big jewellery shops in the area. Yet the TBZ stamp on the bazaar is permanent, and their massive showroom stands out. Customers fly in from all corners of India to own a TBZ original. With more than thirty stores across the country, their legacy is intact. From the days when Bhimji's grandson, Gopaldas created a stir in India's jewellery circles when he introduced the option of a full value gold buy-back scheme to the present time, where fifth-generation customers continue to shop at their stores, it is their policy of 'customer is king', trust, quality and craftsmanship that has kept them on top of their game, over 150 years later.

Other veteran jewellers in this area include Danabhai and Popley for gold, D.P. Zaveri & Sons and Deepchand Sons for silver, and Dwarkadas Chandumal for diamonds.

Where: Opera House, Charni Road

COOL FACT › DARING, UNSOLVED CASE

On March 19, 1987, over twenty conmen entered the famous jewellery store. Led by Mon Singh, they introduced themselves as members of the Central Bureau of Intelligence and Investigation—a non-existent organisation—and flashed a search warrant at the owners. CCTV cameras were ordered to be switched off, the store's licensed revolver was handed over and no telephone calls were allowed while Singh's assistants (hired as 'Security and Intelligence officers' who had answered to a classified ad just a day earlier) collected jewellery samples on the pretext that the its quality had to be checked. At least Rs thirty-five lakh worth of jewellery was stolen during that daring daylight robbery. Singh slunk away with the loot, fooling his assistants and the owners. Despite the Mumbai police pursuing the case, they were unable to catch the mastermind. Over three decades later, the case remains unsolved.

❁ Bibliography ❁

The author would like to acknowledge the following publications, organisations and individuals for their contribution to the research that went into the making of this book:

1 Sharada Dwivedi and Rahul Mehrotra, A City Icon, Eminence Designs, 2006
2 Sharada Dwivedi and Rahul Mehrotra, Bombay, The Cities Within, Eminence Designs, 2001
3 Shaul Sapir, Bombay: Exploring the Jewish Urban Heritage, Bene Israeli Heritage Museum and Geneological Research Centre, India, 2013
4 Christopher London, Bombay Gothic, India Book House, 2002
5 Samuel T Sheppard, Bombay: Places, Names and Street Names, Indus Source Books, 2019
6 Kamu Iyer, Boombay: From Precincts to Sprawl, Popular Prakashan, 2014
7 Behram Contractor, Busybee: The Best of Thirty-Six Years, Penguin India, 2002
8 Gillian Tindall, City of Gold: The Biography of Bombay, Penguin India, 1992
9 George Michell, Elephanta, Deccan Heritage Foundation, 2002
10 Mona and Manju Mehra, Foy Nissen: A Quiet Genius, Mona and Manju Mehra, 2017
11 Rajendra B Aklekar, Halt Station India, Rupa Publications, 2014
12 Monsignor Francis Correa, Heritage of Mount Mary Bandra, Rector, Mount Mary's Basilica, 2004
13 Marriam Dossal, Mumbai: Theatre of Conflict, City of Hope, Mumbai, Oxford University Press, 2010
14 Edited by Manjiri Kamat, Mumbai Past and Present, Indus Source Books, 2014
15 Edited by Lakshmi Subramanian, Ports, Towns, Cities: A Historical Tour of the Indian Littoral, Marg Publications, 2008

16 Gavin Ambrose, Paul Harris and Sally Stone, The Visual Dictionary of Architecture, AVA Publishing, Switzerland, 2008

17 Dr Fleur D'Souza, Witness, Published by the Parish Priest, St John The Baptist Church, Thane, 2018

18 Edited by Kamala Ganesh, Usha Thakkar and Gita Chadha, Zero Point Bombay: In And Around Horniman Circle, Lotus Collection, Roli Books, 2008

19 Tasneem Zakaria Mehta, The Restoration and Revitalisation of Dr Bhau Daji Lad Mumbai City Museum, Managing Trustee for the Museum, 2009

❁ Other Sources ❁

- Art Deco Trust Mumbai
- Asiatic Society of Mumbai official website
- Archives of Deepak Rao, historian
- Archives of Vikas Dilawari Architects
- Archives of Professor Mary Norman Woods, Cornell University
- Archives of Brinda Somaya and Nandini Somaya Sampat
- Archives of Robert Stephens
- Archives of Clayton Murzello
- Archive.org/ Full text of The Memoirs of Field-Marshal The Viscount Montgomery of Alamein, K.G.
- Bombay Natural History Society official website
- Bombay Samachar official website
- BDL Museum official website
- Biodiversity Heritage Library
- Central Railway's official statistics report, February 2021
- Collection.nam.ac.uk
- CSMVS Museum official website
- History.com

- Indianrailways.gov.in (Conservation Plan for Bandra Station)
- Indian Navy official website
- Jehangir Art Gallery official website
- Live History India website
- Lovji Nusserwanjee Wadia by Frederic P Miller, Agnes F Vandome and John McBrewster
- Mumbai dabbawala official website
- Mumbai Cricket Association official website
- Mangroves.maharashtra.gov.in
- Nationalarchives.gov.uk
- Oxford University Press
- Royal Western India Turf Club official website
- Royal Opera House official website
- Salim Ali Centre for Ornithology and Natural History (SACON)
- Salvation.church.in
- Scaarchitects.in/project/marinedrive
- The Zaveri family
- The Eponym Dictionary of Birds by Bo Beolens, Michael Watkins and Michael Grayson
- Theory.tifr.res.in
- Urban Development Research Institute (UDRI)
- News articles from Mid-day, Mumbai, The Times of India, Hindustan Times, Business Standard, Indian Express, The Economic Times, The Quint, moneycontrol.com, The Guardian UK

❁ Glossary of Terms ❁

Architecture and Related Terms

Neoclassical: One of the earliest architectural styles that arrived in India from the West in the early nineteenth century, it is most visible in the Asiatic Society (Town Hall) of Mumbai. Its striking features includes symmetry, horizontality, grandeur of scale, simplicity of exteriors, geometric forms, huge and dramatic use of columns, and a preference for blank walls relieved with rectangular openings and supporting pediments. Another noticeable feature of this style is the absence of detailed carvings or sculpture on its facades, a contrast to Gothic architecture that was the next definitive style to take over Bombay's public buildings.

Neo Gothic: This Gothic architectural style developed in Europe from 1200-mid 1500s to create dramatic monumental buildings. Tall buildings, accentuated with towers and spires, with buttresses (normal and flying), pointed arches, impressive windows and stained glass work and gargoyles, as well as the use of ashlar stone façades, were definitive features of this style. It adapted itself to local conditions wherever used, and hence was visible in structures built in the city in the second half of the nineteenth century. Commissioned architects like F.W. Stevens incorporated it in their facades, most notably for Victoria Terminus (today's Chhatrapati Shivaji Maharaj Terminus) and the Municipal Corporation building.

Two sub-types visible in the city's buildings:

• **Venetian Gothic:** A direct influence of Venice's Gothic architecture, it is visible in sections of the David Sassoon Library and Elphinstone Building; traces of this style can also be spotted in the University Buildings. The style is pronounced with arcaded façades (interlacing arches) and different coloured stones, allowing for direct sunlight that was ideal for Bombay.

• **Victorian Gothic:** Great Britain's Gothic influence, the highpoint of the Victorian Gothic style of architecture, is most visible along the buildings that line Oval Maidan (after the demolition of the Fort walls), including the High Court, University Buildings, City Civil and Sessions Court, Public Works Department and Central Telegraph Office. It is obvious that this style arose from events in Great Britain in the nineteenth century, such as the fire at the Palace of Westminster that housed the British Parliament (1834); the aspiration to introduce a different design, like the new House of Parliament (1840), had taken root in Bombay too. Wide south- and west-facing verandahs to allow ventilation, as well as massive tiled roofed ceilings, to account for hot Indian summers, are some of the standout features. Indian flora and fauna displays on the outer and inner façades of a structure are also typical of this style. This localisation of the style was appreciated by UNESCO when it awarded a World Heritage Site tag to the Victorian Gothic ensemble (facing Oval Maidan). The introduction of the dome in Victoria Terminus (now Chhatrapati Shivaji Maharaj Terminus) was a highlight of this style and later the city of spires became a city of domes.

Indo-Saracenic: This architectural style followed the Gothic movement in the city, and was most visible in buildings that came up in the first half of the twentieth century. Local influences were obvious in the overall character of such buildings. Islamic and Hindu architectural influences like chajjas (projected coverings above windows that offer shade), broad corridors, wide stairways, jali screens, minarets and massive domes and use of regional stone defined this style. The Gateway of India and Prince of Wales Museum (now Chhatrapati Shivaji Maharaj Vastu Sangrahalaya) reflect this style.

Art Deco: This style of architecture emerged from the 1930s onwards, and was the first symbol of a new India. The style echoed the early days of the modernist way of life, in every sense, with soft pastel colours, geometric patterns with symbol elements that were used to represent speed, motion, progress and nautical movement, as well as long balconies and innovative features to adapt to India's tropical climate. It used a new and modern material, concrete as its basic material of construction deviating from stone and timber construction. Indian architects were at the forefront of these new, modern residences, and they did their best to carve a niche in this architectural style. After Miami, Mumbai has the largest collection of Art Deco buildings in the world.

Vernacular (architecture): Local architectural influences, be it traditional motifs or designs, or inspiration from regional building styles and elements used in such homes or structures, like verandahs with tiled roofs and louvres (arrangement of horizontal panels, blades).

Steeple: The highest visible towering element atop a building, often seen in a church. The tapering of the steeple often displayed ornamental design so it could stand out from a distance.

Façade: Exterior front portion of a building, visible to the public eye that typically contains recognisable architectural features and elements. The term has its origins in the French word meaning 'frontage' or 'face'.

Keystone: The central wedge-shaped stone at the top of an arch. It is usually larger than the other wedge-shaped stones (of arches called voussoirs) that create the arch. It was also used to hold the other stones together. In some cases, carvings or sculpting were also done on these keystones.

Conservationist (noun: conservation): A conservationist is a person who advocates conservation of places, structures and sites of heritage and historic value, as well as natural resources like forests and ecosystems.

Amphitheatre: A natural or man-made open space (or closed in some cases), surrounded by seating or rising ground where people can either sit or stand. The central area was used as a stage for public engagement, like a play or an important ceremony.

Stained glass motifs: Pieces of coloured glass that are painted and fired in a kiln and are held by lead cames (slender grooved lead bars used to hold together the panes in stained glass or latticework windows) to collectively create a design motif or a panel. Different panels form a window. Originally seen only in churches, this style extended to public buildings and homes as well. When light passes through it, it displays a stunning brightness and colour to the space. It uses geometric and floral patterns.

UNESCO World Heritage Site: These include areas or objects of outstanding universal value as recognised by the United Nations Educational, Scientific and Cultural Organisation (UNESCO). The intent of identifying these sites is to preserve and protect these cultural and natural treasures across the world from neglect, damage or attacks. This recognition is viewed as a matter of immense honour and pridfe for its home country. This comes with the responsibility to maintain it as per accepted international standards.

UNESCO Asia-Pacific Awards for Cultural Heritage Conservation: Annual honours awarded to (mostly private) restored heritage sites within the Asia and Pacific region that are selected based on pre-determined criteria by UNESCO.

Backbay Reclamation Scheme: In the early part of the twentieth century a serious effort was initiated by the Bombay Government to reclaim land from the sea by the western shoreline. This led to the creation of the Backbay Reclamation Scheme, and, under it, building plans for modern residences along today's Marine Drive and Churchgate, began to be laid out, thus giving the city's residential buildings a new character.

Basalt stone: A type of igneous rock found in western India that is strong and dense, and hence favoured for construction. Found locally, it is also referred to as Deccan Trap.

Rose window: A circular window with foils of patterned tracery arranged like spokes of a wheel

Gargoyle: A carved shape of an animal or a demon protruding from the façade of a building that drains out rain water, away from the sides of the walls. It has its origins in medieval Europe and was often used in church design, to ward off evil spirits due to its scary forms.

Roundel: A small circular decorative plate that often has the carved face of a person and is placed in as the niche of a façade

General Terms / Phrases

Datum: A reference or a starting point from where calculations or measurements are taken

Antiquities: Term used to define relics, remains, coins and other items of heritage value from the distant past

Impregnable: One that cannot be conquered; usually mentioned in context of a fort or a high wall

Six sigma code: A process oriented methodology that is designed to improve business performance. Mumbai's dabbawalas use this system to ensure minimum chance for errors in the delivery of the lunchboxes (dabbas) to lakhs of customers across the city on a daily basis.

Quaker: Belonging to a Christian religious group (In the context of Mark Twain's reference—he calls the Indian crow a 'sham quaker'–someone who cannot be trusted; a fraudster)

Causeway: A raised pathway or road over a wet, marshy land or water body. Two of the main causeways that connected early Bombay with its suburbs were built at Mahim and Sion, on the western and eastern sides, respectively.

Traffic island: A construction or an installation in the middle of a busy junction meant to separate movement in different directions.

Admiralty: The officials or the department of state having charge of naval affairs. In context of Bombay, the British Admiralty was a government department that was responsible for the command of the Royal Navy until 1964.

Basilica: An important place of worship in Christianity; it is usually a large and important church where special rights are conferred by the spiritual head, the Pope.

Weathervane: A revolving pointer to show the direction of the wind; most likely to be spotted atop a building.

Plaque: A commemorative, decorative memorial of a person who has passed away or of an event, that is made from metal, marble, wood or porcelain.

Pier: A structure built on posts extending from land out over water, used as a landing place for ships to dock and for the use of passengers and crew.

Franciscan: A priest, nun, or lay member of a Christian religious order founded in 1209 by St Francis of Assisi or based on its rule, and noted for its preachers and missionaries

Resurrection: A Biblical occurrence that refers to Jesus Christ rising from the dead on the third day after he was crucified on the cross

Promenade: A paved pathway that lines a river or the sea

Grotto: A cave-like space, either natural or manmade, often used to place a religious statue or idol

Local Terms

Pali language: Pali is one of the ancient languages in India. The Buddha had chosen Pali for his teachings since he felt it was the common man's language. It was phased out in most parts of India by the fourteenth century.

Brun: This is a crusty, round-shaped pav that has a soft centre but is different in texture from naram (soft pav). The reason for its difference is that it is steam-baked. A popular entry in most menus of Irani cafés, it is best eaten with butter or jam to accompany tea.

Berry pulao: The only place in India that serves this dish in its authentic version is Britannia in Ballard Estate. Conceptualised by Bachan, wife of the iconic restaurateur late Boman Kohinoor in 1982, this pulao is made of soft rice, flavoured with saffron, tender mutton or chicken and its pièce-de-résistance, the Irani zereshk berries (sour barberries).

Dhansak: One of the most popular dishes of Parsi Zoroastrian cuisine, used to be traditionally served on the fourth day after the death of a near one. Mutton or goat meat is cooked in a mixture of lentils and vegetables to form a mush. The dish is served with caramelised rice, and is now a common feature on most Irani restaurant and café menus.

Lagan nu custard: As the name suggests, this is a special custard made at weddings (lagan: wedding/Gujarati). Made with milk, eggs, butter and nuts, the addition of sultanas, cashews, almonds and pistachios gives it a rich consistency. This dessert is a Sunday treat in Parsi homes.

Patra ni machi: A specialty that features in every Parsi celebration, pomfret fish is marinated in spices and salt, slathered with a green paste chutney and wrapped in banana leaves before being steamed.

Koliwada: Koli—fisher folk of Mumbai; wada—traditionally, a cluster of homes built in local, vernacular style, usually belonging to members of a particular community or profession. Mumbai is home to koliwadas where members of the Koli community live and practise their profession, i.e., fishing. Most of these clusters line the city's coastline. Some of the surviving koliwadas are located in Worli, Versova and near Cuffe Parade in South Mumbai.

Malabar teak: Teakwood sourced from the Malabar Coast, which geographically falls along Kerala's coastline. This wood is termed as a strong type, used for heavy-duty construction, from structures to ships.

❁ Acknowledgements ❁

THIS book would not have been possible without guides, influencers, guardian angels and well-wishers who have been a part of my life, especially during this 'return journey' to releasing a title after fifteen years.

Hemali Sodhi, my literary agent, for being godmother to this book. You believed in an idea from a time-strapped newspaper journalist who had dashed across a few offbeat briefs one September night in the lockdown, and gave it wings. Ambar Sahil Chatterjee, co-advisor, your practical and timely advice as the book took shape ensured every hurdle was crossed smoothly.

My editor Tina Narang, you've been the archetypal Aesopian owl, offering wisdom and direction as I returned to the challenging world of writing a book. Ananth Padmanabhan and the support teams at HarperCollins, your presence and input have been rock solid. A shoutout to Bonita Vaz-Shimray and Ankita Deshpande for your investment in this project. Shamika Chaves, thank you for waving your magic wand over the book's cover; it's the perfect sumptuous teaser for what's inside!

Sumedha Sah, you introduced life, colour, emotion and a certain Bombay-ness, typical to this vibrant city with your illustrations, all the while staying honest to the core and intent of this book.

Pradnya Naik, your clean and intelligent design did full justice to translate and weave text and visuals into a symphonic jugalbandi.

My mentors, Deepak Rao, city historian, and Vikas Dilawari, UNESCO award-winning architect and conservationist, I am grateful for your time and effort to painstakingly read my manuscript, and offer invaluable feedback.

Sowmya Venkat, 'da boss', for all things history, heritage and Bombay; only the universe would be able to trace when you planted the seed for this book in my head. You've been fabulous along every turn of this book.

Tinaz Nooshian, Mid-day's editor-in-chief, your 'heritage can be cool' mantra, amplified by writings in the newspaper, tapri chai breaks and wanderings to explore off-the-grid Bombay, reignited my urge to bring this subject to a wider audience.Being the ever-present sounding board with Buddha-like calm ensured this was a smooth sign-off.

Preeti Nair, I cherish the countless moments, from monologues over Udipi breakfasts as idyllic collegians, to probing chats over TV dinners as battle-hardened professionals; several such sessions triggered countless leaps of faith, including writing this book.

Brinda Somaya, UNESCO award-winning architect and conservationist; Tasneem Mehta, Managing Director, Dr Bhau Daji Lad Museum; Sabyasachi Mukherjee, Director General, Chhatrapati Shivaji Maharaj Vastu Sangrahalaya; Atul Kumar, Founder-Trustee, Art Deco Mumbai; Professor Mary Woods, Professor Mustansir Dalvi and Professor Fleur D'Souza: your passion for the heritage in this city is infectious; your support over the years, humbling.

Nandini Somaya Sampat, city architect and conservationist, when this book was in the incubation lab, you backed the idea, and gladly agreed for your sons to be my first reviewers. Bijal Vachcharajani, a.k.a 'Agent Vinod', you've been a navigator in your usual understated way. Suhani Singh, your support on this journey where we continue to celebrate Bombay, has been precious. Phorum Pandya, for always being 'game' to jam about the book during our after-hours gupshup. Salaams to Ahalya Naidu and Meethil Momaya, my cheerleader squad at Trilogy, Bandra.

I am thankful to my colleagues in the newsroom—Clayton Murzello, Hemal Ashar, Rajendra B Aklekar, Ranjeet Jadhav and Sukanya Datta for their inputs. Author and columnist Meher Marfatia, your positive review for my previous book was the springboard that kept this heritage buff excited for bigger ideas.

My English schoolteacher Rina Bhattacharya, for spotting a reticent student's passion for writing, and for debunking conventional beliefs that you have to be a Maths or Science wiz to reach for the stars. Dr Rose Davies and Nirmala Nahata, you ensured my equilibrium was in balance as I juggled between pressing newspaper deadlines and this special project.

Much gratitude to my dear friend, the late William Pinto, who all those years ago introduced me to the enchanted world of visual storytelling with his envious collection of Tintin and Asterix comic books. Locksley Peter Fernandez, thank you for introducing a wide-eyed teenager to the delights of Fort's bookstores and secondhand booksellers. The Mollans—Raylene, Conrad and Fenella—I've been blessed to have you as my anchor, my family.

Lastly, but most importantly, my late parents, Beula and Shelton—I am here because of you. Mum, for always backing my ideas, oddball as they were, for letting me be, and for fuelling my curiosity about Bombay, and life, one book at a time. Dad, for showing me the marvels of this city, from VT to the Gateway, in your own bindaas way. And a hat tip for introducing me to the Rafi classic that's now part of my sensibilities and everyday inspiration: 'Bombay Meri Jaan'.

About the Author

Fiona Fernandez is a historian at heart with a time-traveller's soul. As Associate Editor at Mid-day and through her outspoken protagonists Sir PM and Lady Flora, in her weekly column *Bombaynama,* Fiona highlights Mumbai's multi-layered urban histories, the conservation of its UNESCO World Heritage Sites and its citizen champions.

In this book, Fiona brings in a contemporary perspective along with a real-world take on all things heritage. Written with disarming simplicity for the young and the old reader, the book is an exploration of the city's treasures, from its famous sites to its off-beat paths, decrepit buildings, nondescript gullies and charming neighbourhoods. Fiona's eye for detail and rigour of on-ground research is what make this book a tribute to the 'Bombay' brand of resilience.

Fiona has also written *Bombay Meri Jaan* and *Ten Heritage Walks of Mumbai.* She was co-researcher for The Mumbai Factfile and has contributed to *Urban Voice 3* and *The Book of Dog.*

When she isn't writing or strolling about SoBo's streetscapes, Fiona prefers watching reruns of Wimbledon finals, attempting online quizzes or having a thought bubble conversation with a friendly stray.

❉ About the Illustrator ❉

Born in Nainital, Sumedha is an architect with a specialization in sustainable architecture, and a self-taught illustrator. She has a keen interest in the ever-evolving man–nature relationship. Her art and illustrations have appeared in several publications in India and abroad. As an architect, she co-designed the Railway Museum in Mysore, which opened to the public in March 2022. She loves to take leisurely nature walks, cook hearty meals, travel to lesser-known destinations, write long letters and draw in her sketchbooks. She especially enjoys creating books for children. She lives and works out of her studio in Bangalore. This is her tenth book.

30 Years *of*

HarperCollins*Publishers*India

At HarperCollins, we believe in telling the best stories and finding the widest possible readership for our books in every format possible. We started publishing 30 years ago; a great deal has changed since then, but what has remained constant is the passion with which our authors write their books, the love with which readers receive them, and the sheer joy and excitement that we as publishers feel in being a part of the publishing process.

Over the years, we've had the pleasure of publishing some of the finest writing from the subcontinent and around the world, and some of the biggest bestsellers in India's publishing history. Our books and authors have won a phenomenal range of awards, and we ourselves have been named Publisher of the Year the greatest number of times. But nothing has meant more to us than the fact that millions of people have read the books we published, and somewhere, a book of ours might have made a difference.

As we step into our fourth decade, we go back to that one word – a word which has been a driving force for us all these years.

Read.